TIME

—— *Hugh Sidey's* ——

PORTRAITS

OF THE

PRESIDENTS

HUGH SIDEY'S PORTRAITS OF THE PRESIDENTS

Editor	Kelly Knauer
Writer	Hugh Sidey
Art Director	Ellen Fanning
Picture Editor	Patricia Cadley
Copy Editor	Bruce Christopher Carr
Editorial Research	Deirdre Van Dyk, Mary Hart
Production Director	John Calvano
Photo Technology	Urbano Delvalle
TIME Special Projects Editor	Barrett Seaman

Thanks to: Dick Duncan, Ed Jamieson, Betty Satterwhite Sutter, Cornelis Verwaal

TIME INC. HOME ENTERTAINMENT

President	Stuart Hotchkiss
Executive Director, Branded Businesses	David Arfine
Executive Director, Non Branded Businesses	Alicia Longobardo
Executive Director, Time Inc. Brand Licensing	Risa Turken
Director, Licensing	Scott Rosenzweig
Executive Director, Marketing Services	Carol Pittard
Director, Retail & Special Sales	Tom Mifsud
Director, Branded Businesses	Maarten Terry
Associate Directors	Roberta Harris, Kenneth Maehlum
Product Managers	Dana Gregory, Andre Okolowitz, Ann Marie Ross, Niki Viswanathan, Daria Raehse
Associate Product Managers	Victoria Alfonso, Jennifer Dowell, Dennis Sheehan, Meredith Shelley, Lauren Zaslansky
Assistant Product Managers	Ann Gillespie, Meredith Peters, Virginia Valdes
Telemarketing Manager	Marina Weinstein
Associate Manager, e-Commerce	Dima Masrizada
Licensing Manager	Joanna West
Associate Licensing Manager	Regina Feiler
Licensing Coordinator	Laury Shapiro
Associate Manager, Retail & New Markets	Bozena Szwagulinski
Coordinator, Retail Marketing	Gina Di Meglio
Editorial Operations Director	John Calvano
Assitant Editorial Operations Manager	Emily Rabin
Book Production Manager	Jessica McGrath
Associate Book Production Manager	Jonathan Polsky
Assistant Book Production Manager	Suzanne DeBenedetto
Fulfillment Manager	Richard Perez
Assistant Fulfillment Manager	Tara Schimming
Financial Director	Tricia Griffin
Financial Manager	Robert Dente
Associate Financial Manager	Steven Sandonato
Assistant Financial Manager	Tamara Whittier
Executive Assistant	Mary Jane Rigoroso

Copyright 2000 by Time Inc. Home Entertainment
Published by TIME Books
Time Inc., 1271 Ave. of the Americas, New York, NY 10020

Library of Congress: 00-101243
ISBN: 1-929049-04-8

We welcome your comments and suggestions about TIME Books. Please write to us at:

TIME Books
Attention: Book Editors
P.O. Box 11016
Des Moines, IA 50336-1016

To order additional copies, please call 1-800-327-6388
(Monday through Friday 7:00 a.m.—8:00 p.m. or Saturday 7:00 a.m.—6:00 p.m. Central Time)

Printed in the United States of America

TIME

Hugh Sidey's

PORTRAITS
OF THE
PRESIDENTS

Power and Personality in the Oval Office

CONTENTS

OUR MAN IN WASHINGTON Hugh Sidey peeks out from behind his perch at John F. Kennedy's Inauguration on January 20, 1961

INTRODUCTION

"What Do I Do Now?"

By Hugh Sidey

AFTER AN ASSERTIVE CAMPAIGN OF PROMISES TO "GET America moving again," the victorious John Kennedy was ensconced in the Oval Office with a small but joyful ritual the morning after his Inauguration. Staff members then quietly departed and left the new President alone. The story goes that aide Ralph Dungan was immediately summoned back by the President. Apprehensively opening the door of the office, he was greeted by a grinning Kennedy. "What do I do now?" he asked.

That was a flash of the famous Kennedy wit, and also a reminder that no person entering that office is quite sure how to begin his journey. I felt much the same way when I began writing about Presidents more than 40 years ago, in 1957.

The nine men I covered were alike in that they were triumphant political figures, but they were wildly differing human beings, whose leadership styles were shaped by their individual characters and backgrounds. Many of my initial impressions of them were wrong, for mine was a constant voyage of learning and correcting my views. I can recall shivering in front of the U.S. Capitol on a sodden day in January as Dwight Eisenhower took the oath of office for his second term. Fresh out of New York City, I was a correspondent for the weekly LIFE magazine. The presidency seemed so simple then. We had a man in office who had led the Allied armies in Europe to victory. He had known and worked with Franklin Roosevelt, Winston Churchill and Charles de Gaulle. He had gathered in his Administration strong, successful people from academe, law, banking and business. The U.S. had a huge portion of the world's wealth and much of its military might. I was quite convinced that I knew most of the answers concerning how a President should go about his duties.

Since then we have been through more than a score of wars and military actions, three assassinations of major national figures, three attempts on the lives of Presidents, half a dozen economic recessions, a scandal that forced a President to resign, civil-rights struggles, dozens of natural calamities and terrorist acts, the end of the cold war and, finally, the impeachment and exoneration of President Bill Clinton.

Through all the turmoil, the purposes and ideals of the presidency have remained constant, though the men at times have faltered, and all were deeply influenced by the rush of events. As I stand now in a city that has grown familiar to me and survey the presidency, I am far less certain about the combination of qualities that makes a successful national steward, and I invoke fewer rigid measures of both ability and achievement. A President can be lifted up or beaten down by other world leaders totally out of his sphere of influence. And he can be inspired or discouraged by the times in which he presides. The cauldron of the presidency reveals unknown strengths in a person, just as it exposes hidden weaknesses.

In Ronald Reagan's last year in office, I was approached in London by a political student curious about the presidency and the men who had served recently. "Your last President was a peanut farmer who once ran a nuclear submarine, and this one was an old sports announcer who became a grade-B Hollywood actor," he pointed out, then asked, "Where do you get these chaps?" That was a telling gibe from a young man whose nation has a backup government at all times trained and in place. Yet the very diversity of our Presidents has been a strength as well as a weakness. We have found amazing virtuosity in out-of-the-way places such as Springfield, Illinois, where Abraham Lincoln practiced country law. But we also have found that the worldly Herbert Hoover, the most intelligent and experienced public servant of his age, was ill-suited to stem the ravages of the Great Depression.

There is no tried and true training course for this role— "No handbook for the job," Kennedy once told me. His first year included a series of tough lessons, from the Bay of Pigs to the Berlin Wall. Nearly 30 years later, George Bush opened the middle drawer of his Oval Office desk when he first

moved in and found a note from Ronald Reagan. "Don't let the turkeys get you down," was the heading on the small pad, which had the profile of a turkey. "You'll have moments when you want to use this particular stationery," Reagan wrote in a firm hand. "Well, go to it." Bush had attended most of the important Reagan policy meetings over eight years, had lunched regularly with the President. Still, when Bush became President and was confronted with the savings and loan scandal and the outlaw governments in Panama and Iraq, he found he had no clear set of procedures to follow, either written down or passed along in talks with Reagan.

Many of Bush's important decisions, like those of other Presidents, rested in varying degrees on intuition, the quality former Secretary of State Henry Kissinger called one of the crucial ingredients of leadership. He insisted that in almost every moment of presidential decision there is never enough of the right information at precisely the right time. A President, Kissinger said, almost always had to leap across a last void and make judgments on his gut feeling—on intuition, a mystical mix of experience, intelligence and hope. A subject that only vaguely occurred to Lyndon Johnson, for instance, got the attention of Richard Nixon: he reached out to the People's Republic of China, an adversary for 22 years and a frequent target of his own denunciations. Sadly, Nixon's instincts were far less acute when it came to domestic politics, and he was driven from office by the Watergate scandal.

Jimmy Carter seemed paralyzed at times by his awareness that he did not have all the information he sought for a given decision. He went to prodigious lengths to gather facts, to digest and order them. He hesitated in confronting inflation and high interest rates, and he ended up with both evils, which the economists called "stagflation." That came after the voters had banished Gerald Ford, in part because he had pardoned Nixon, an intuitive act that Ford felt was necessary to get Watergate behind us. It may have hurt Ford politically, but such courage gets Ford a good note in the history books.

Ronald Reagan was certainly never overburdened by detail on any day of his presidency. Nor did he want to be. But I believe he had developed a good ration of intuition in his long life. The full sweep of all the history he had seen and lived was in his heart and mind.

In many ways, Lyndon Johnson is the most fascinating creature of the modern presidency. I use the word creature purposely, because Washington was Johnson's preserve and he was king of the beasts. He was probably the best legislator the country has ever had. He knew the bank balances and philanderings of his enemies, understood the family relationships of his allies. But when L.B.J. ventured very far beyond the continental U.S., he faltered. He had neither traveled much nor read extensively about other countries. He had not been a student of foreign policy when he was in the Senate. His finely honed Capitol Hill instincts did not apply to war and diplomacy, and Vietnam consumed him.

THE PRESIDENCY REMAINS THE MOST SOUGHT-AFTER, analyzed and scrutinized political office man has devised. We have poked and peered at each succeeding President with increased ferocity. I well recall my first briefing around the desk of Jim Hagerty, Ike's press secretary. There were no more than 12 White House correspondents, and when told there would be no news that day, we all drifted off to lunch and other pursuits.

Now there can be as many as a hundred correspondents on routine news days, each looking for some fragment that can be built into a story for the evening broadcasts, the morning newspapers or the instant Internet. With the advent of television, the President has become the central player in a world spectacle, not only the wielder of the terrible swift sword, guardian of the purse, arbiter of good and evil, but also the star of a giant soap opera, complete with wife, kids, dogs and a big house full of guests. President-watching remains an intriguing, often surprising and dramatic business.

With each new President we probe deeper and we learn more. And yet the final analysis of the human soul still eludes us, thank goodness. As for myself, give me a man or woman with common sense, a passion for fair play, a knowledge of his or her nation and the world, an itch for adventure, a touch of romance about his or her role and a good dash of boldness, and I think we will fare quite well. When a President with some of those qualities understands his own special strengths and can admit his weaknesses, burnishing the former and avoiding the latter, we can expect greatness in the Oval Office. ∎

Third Inauguration, Washington, 1941

Franklin Delano Roosevelt

America was mired in depression as fascism took root abroad—until a disabled man rallied a paralyzed nation

THE MEANING AND THE IMAGE OF PRESIDENT Franklin D. Roosevelt grow stronger as time passes. In a recent C-SPAN survey, American historians ranked him above George Washington on their list of great Presidents; he is now No. 2, just below Abraham Lincoln, who, like Roosevelt, preserved the United States ("The last best hope of earth") in extreme crisis.

From someplace deep within Roosevelt came bold and unshakable confidence in the American people. He understood that this free land possessed limitless resources to be marshaled against the great depression and then the Nazi tyranny, which plunged much of the globe into World War II. If there was a blazing banner under which he strode and summoned the country behind him, it was spoken in his first Inaugural Address on a cold, dreary day in 1933: "The only thing we have to fear is fear itself."

Nothing seemed to daunt him, and that showed in a large face that radiated humor and strength ("There is nothing I love as much as a good fight") and a rich baritone that resonated through every corner of the nation. As radio networks matured, they became the handmaiden of a President who under-

stood the new power of bringing his voice inside each home and talking as if he were a family friend.

Roosevelt relished the stage he had created. One of his aides, Thomas Corcoran, once told me that F.D.R.'s preparations for a "fireside chat" were little short of a star getting ready for a climactic movie scene. Roosevelt gargled profusely, summoned a Navy corpsman to minister to his vocal cords and sinuses with swabs and sprays. He then read a few of his best lines to staff members for critical assessment. Given the radio signal, "Ladies and gentlemen, the President of the United Sates," Roosevelt, according to Corcoran, was emotionally transported abroad in the country, seeing and feeling in his mind the people to whom he was talking. He was there–and his listeners knew it.

I was a young boy in western Iowa in those desperate years of depression and drought. I was too young to understand what was at stake when Roosevelt talked on the radio, and so I would take refuge with my friends in the front yards up and down our street. What I vividly remember is that as we wandered from yard to yard in the scorching summer months, I could hear from inside each house the President's voice, and I could see through the open windows the parents of my friends all huddled around their radios. Americans had never been closer together.

Then there were the pictures—tens of thousands of pictures that bloomed in the dawning of our visual age; pictures in the scratchy frames of newsreels on the screens in movie houses, on the front pages of the newspapers, later in the glossy spreads of LIFE and *Look* magazines. There he was in his open touring car in a floppy felt hat joking with farmers in the heat of the dust bowl, once again bringing hope where a

intrusive. Few people believe it will ever shrink. Most people believe it is necessary for a nation of 270 million people.

When I arrived in 1957, Washington was still under the cloak of Roosevelt. Many of the bureaucrats from his time remained there. His aides had stayed in town to be lawyers and consultants, advising new Presidents and dealing with Congress. Members of the press who had covered his long reign still told stories of the old days with deep feelings. On one of those endless jet trips with later Presidents, I recall Richard Wilson, of the Cowles publications, relating how he had been sent to Washington to cover Secretary of Agriculture Henry Wallace, one of the true innovators in the New Deal. "Every day there was something new out of the Department of Agriculture to try to deal with the farm crisis," explained Wilson. "It was the most exciting place in the most exciting time in Washington." And many of the brilliant people who worked there would in later years have a profound effect on American life. Their disparate likes included lawyer and presidential adviser Abe Fortas and the onetime trusted aide to Under Secretary of State Dean Acheson, Alger Hiss, who later was accused of being a communist spy and was convicted of perjury.

I got one of my most poignant insights into Roosevelt and his times one evening some years ago from West Virginia Senator Jennings Randolph, who claimed he was the last living member of Congress who was on the Inaugural stand when F.D.R. took his first oath of office. "I remember it as if it was yesterday," he told me. "It was a gray, cold day. I was a new Congressman from West Virginia and I was scared to death.

As radio networks matured, they became the handmaiden of a President who undersood the new power of bringing his voice inside each home and talking as if among friends … Americans had never been closer together

few years before there was none. He was pictured with his outlandish cigarette holder at a rakish angle, somehow with F.D.R. a symbol of confidence and not a dilettante's fetish. With a cape thrown over his shoulders on the deck of a destroyer, the sea wind in his hair, he was the bold and beloved Commander in Chief.

Pictures of Roosevelt, the polio victim, in his wheelchair were not circulated. He had asked the press not to show him as disabled, though he spent his days in the wheelchair and could only walk a few steps with leg braces. The press scrupulously honored his request. Most Americans had no idea of the extent of their President's disability. Those who knew admired his courage all the more.

Roosevelt created the modern Federal Government, big departments in huge gray buildings sprawling across the heart of the capital, to this day still a part of the debate on whether the government is too big, too expensive and too

We all sat on that stand made of raw lumber and huddled in our overcoats wondering if this country would survive the economic collapse. Everybody I knew had lost faith in the system. To be honest, I wasn't expecting much. Then President Roosevelt began to speak. I tell you, it changed the world. That voice of his filled the Capitol grounds, and I think that everyone took heart. He was so optimistic, so upbeat. After that speech we would have given him any power he wanted; we would have made him dictator had he asked."

Another time I was walking down a White House corridor with President Lyndon Johnson, who was worrying about Vietnam, when we came up to a bust of Roosevelt. Johnson, who had been one of F.D.R.'s devout supporters in Congress, suddenly stopped and changed the subject. He was back 30 years. He went over to the bust, took the bronze chin in his hand and stroked it. *"There* was a man," he said. "Look at that chin. Look at how fearless he was. Look at his courage." ■

1884

1904

A Study in Courage

1920

1932

1944

CHILDHOOD Franklin Roosevelt was born on January 30, 1882. His mother, the former Sara Delano, was the second wife of the much older James Roosevelt, a fourth cousin of Theodore Roosevelt's. James had inherited a great deal of money; Franklin was raised in grand fashion on a large estate in Hyde Park, New York, on the Hudson River.

MARRIAGE Eleanor Roosevelt was Franklin's sixth cousin; they married in 1904. Serious of mind and liberal in her politics, she would become a trusted and active political partner throughout F.D.R.'s career, even though their marriage was shattered in September 1918 when Eleanor learned that Franklin had been carrying on a love affair with her social secretary, Lucy Mercer.

CANDIDATE After making his name in Washington as Assistant Secretary of the Navy, F.D.R. achieved wide recognition when he ran as the Democratic nominee for Vice President on the ticket with James M. Cox; at left, they're campaigning in Dayton, Ohio. Republicans Warren G. Harding and Calvin Coolidge easily defeated the Democrats in the election.

VICTIM Polio struck F.D.R. in 1921 at his summer home at Campobello, New Brunswick, Canada. At left he does "hydrogymnastics" at Warm Springs, Georgia. Hailing F.D.R. in 1940, TIME said one key to his strength was that "no one has ever heard him admit that he cannot walk."

FOUR-TIME WINNER In November 1944, Roosevelt celebrated his fourth election to the presidency, welcoming neighbors who had staged a torchlight parade to his Hyde Park home. Though his health had sharply declined, TIME said before the election, "The Old Master still had it ... a perfection of timing and tone, and an assurance that no young player, no matter how gifted, can equal."

1930

1941

A World of Want and War

America's longest-serving President battled economic woes at home and fascism abroad

1933

1938

1939

HARD TIMES: "This generation of Americans has a rendezvous with destiny," said Franklin Roosevelt in 1936. He took office in 1933 during one of the darkest periods in U.S. history: four years after the stock-market crash of 1929 had sent many into the slums known as "Hoovervilles" (top left), the economy was collapsing, banks were closing and panic was setting in. Yet after four years of the New Deal, F.D.R. said in 1937, "I see one-third of a nation ill-housed, ill-clad, ill-nourished." Two years later, many Americans still lived in poverty (at left is a Dorothea Lange picture of a South Dakota family that had come to California seeking work).

Even as F.D.R. fought the Depression, the events that would draw the U.S. into World War II were taking shape abroad. In February 1933, Adolf Hitler became Chancellor of Germany. In 1931 the Japanese invaded Manchuria (above), putting them on a collision course with the U.S. and Britain in the Pacific. On December 7, 1941, the Japanese sank the battleship U.S.S. *Arizona* (top center) in the surprise attack on the U.S. naval base at Pearl Harbor in Hawaii. The "day that will live in infamy," in F.D.R.'s words, plunged the U.S. into war.

Washington: Rites of Passage

As long as they lived, these old Roosevelt warriors never lost their zest. I concluded that they were a special breed of young men and women when they joined the New Deal. Bold gamblers, they were willing to risk a good chunk of their youth, but they believed the cause of bringing dignity and well-being to America was worth the throw. Their gamble paid off, and what's more— they had fun.

THE TITLE OF BEN COHEN'S SPEECH THE OTHER night was "The New Deal Looks Forward." It was as if Franklin Roosevelt were still in the White House and his staff members were rolling up their sleeves for another job.

Friday was the 44th anniversary of Roosevelt's first Inauguration, and some 750 of the men and women who went into power with him, or joined later, or were otherwise specially touched by those years, came together at

NEW DEALERS Ben Cohen and Tommy Corcoran share smiles in their heyday, left, and at the 1977 reunion

Washington's Mayflower Hotel in commemoration. Cohen, 82, one of F.D.R.'s ubiquitous counselors and trouble-shooters, sounded the theme of marching on. Indeed, the New Deal in flesh and emotion and philosophy does seem to go on forever. It may have been the most dramatic change in government in our history. "It was," explained Thomas G. ("Tommy the Cork") Corcoran, "the institutionalization of compassion."

For a night they drank and laughed and told stories, old people grown young again, those who had hustled into Washington with their cardboard suitcases, frayed clothes, new law degrees and fresh hope.

On that March 4 in 1933, Corcoran, then just 32, was standing in the cold about a hundred feet out in the audience below Roosevelt. He was a young lawyer working for President Herbert Hoover in the Reconstruction Finance Corporation, trying to save the banks. At 1 o'clock on that day Roosevelt's voice echoed over the Capitol Plaza: "The only thing we have to fear is fear itself."

Corcoran stood there knowing that the banks would soon be closed and wondering whether Roosevelt's action would give Americans a sense of confidence or send them into a panic. It was one of the great leadership gambles of history. Corcoran, from his inside position, had wrestled with the personal problem of whether to take his money out of his bank or leave it in. He told the story with relish—how he met the devil halfway, took half of his money out and left half of it in the bank.

West Virginia's Senator Jennings Randolph joined exuberantly in the nostalgia bath. At 30, he had been a new Congressman, seated up on the inaugural stand just 35 feet from Roosevelt. Randolph is the only legislator from F.D.R.'s first 100 days who still is in Congress. He recalled how he had been invited to the White House a few nights later with other new Congressmen. When someone suggested the President was moving too fast, Roosevelt doubled his fist and struck his desk twice. "I still can see how his knuckles got white," said Randolph. "Roosevelt answered, 'But gentlemen, do you realize that we must act now. By acting now we will make mistakes, but if we do not act now, we may not have another opportunity to act at all.'"

The aging New Dealers all recalled with relish how Walter Lippmann, the prominent pundit, had dismissed Roosevelt as "a pleasant man who, without any important qualifications for the office, would like very much to be President." The thing that had saved Roosevelt, the New Dealers insisted, was that he did not have the least idea how things got done. He just decided what needed to be done and left it to others to achieve the impossible. Thus unburdened with technicalities, the President made it to cocktail time each day with his hope still intact. The country got the message.

What fun it had all been. Rex Tugwell, at 85 the oldest of the Roosevelt originals, marveled at their ability to laugh in those dismal times. Then he chuckled over the memory of seeing Tammany Democrats dressed in their long coats and plug hats but so broke they could not pay their hotel bills. "We didn't understand the seriousness of the problem," mused Tommy the Cork, still young at 76, "but we knew the joy of functioning." ∎

A Monumental Mistake

Old prejudices die hard and so did the conviction with some Roosevelt family members and supporters that F.D.R.'s desire not to be shown in the 1930s in a wheel-chair should be carried forth in the Roosevelt memorial of our time. The original design had no depiction of his dis-ability. Historians and other critics argued that if Roosevelt were alive now, he would be the first to insist on an honest look at his condition. Happily, family and friends changed their view, and public and private money was raised for a sculpture of F.D.R. in his wheelchair to be placed at the entrance to the monument.

THEY CAME HUMBLY AND QUIETLY LAST WEEK IN wheelchairs and with leader dogs and a sign-language interpreter, hopeful paraplegic old men, and vigorous middle-age people except for their weakened limbs and dimmed eyes, and glowing young-sters with silence in their ears.

They were a coterie representing 50 million disabled Americans who were invited by the U.S. Park Service to preview the sprawling monument for Franklin Roosevelt to be dedicated May 2. The monument spreads out grandly on 7.5 acres along Washington's Tidal Basin, great blocks of ocher South Dakota granite carved with the soaring phrases of F.D.R.'s that brought this nation through eco-nomic collapse and war.

But in the $48 million monument there is no depiction of Roosevelt in the wheelchair he used for 24 years, noth-ing in the gardens and along the pathways to show his dis-ability at a glance for those who remember and for children who never knew the personal struggle that shaped him.

The small vanguard of disabled people left the site sad-dened, believing to a person that the monument seemed lifeless, lacking the heroic vibrancy of Roosevelt with his radiant smile, head back, steering himself into that des-tiny he saw beyond all adversity. "The essence of the man is missing," said wheelchair user Mike Deland, chairman of the National Organization on Disability. And a handful of Gallaudet College students agreed in sign language, declaring the monument to be incomplete history as they had learned it and saying they would join a demonstration planned for the dedication day.

Mick Countee sensed the emptiness because after he broke his neck in a diving accident, while he was a Harvard student, his mother told him, "Son, if Franklin Roosevelt could be President, you can finish your educa-tion." Countee, who is black, not only finished but also earned a law degree from Georgetown and an M.B.A. from Harvard. "Not a day went by," he said last week, "that I did not think of Roosevelt and Roy Campanella." Campa-nella was the Brooklyn Dodgers catcher who was para-lyzed in a car accident but never despaired in public.

Jim Dickson, the man organizing the demonstration, stood nearly sightless along the huge monument walls and imagined how a statue of Roosevelt in a wheelchair at the entrance would bring the stone to life. When Dickson was seven, he was told by his doctor that he had juvenile

CAPED CRUSADER Advocates for the disabled protested that F.D.R. was not seated in a wheelchair in this sculpture

macular degeneration and would soon be blind. As he walked with his parents out of the doctor's office, his mother told him, "If Franklin Roosevelt, who had polio and was in a wheelchair, could be President, then you can do what you want." He never forgot.

This cry for understanding from the disabled commu-nity is being heard. At least 16 Roosevelt family members now seek a design alteration. A press conference at a foundry casting some of the sculptures was halted by a protest. Another demonstration is planned around the San Francisco office of monument designer Lawrence Halprin.

Former Presidents Bush, Ford and Carter have urged an additional sculpture to show Roosevelt in a wheelchair, and Bush has sent off a "Dear Bill" note to Clinton in hopes he can encourage a peace before Clinton gives the dedication address. Meanwhile every historian of conse-quence who has considered the issue has concluded that the monument is a tragic misreading of the spirit of Franklin D. Roosevelt and a grave misstatement of history for the generations to come.   ■

THE PEOPLE'S CHOICE

It's an irony of the office: candidates for the presidency crisscross the land, taking the voters' pulse in dozens of doughnut shops, across scores of rope lines and in hundreds of hotel ballrooms. But once they reach the White House, that tangible link with the people is cut. Is it any wonder that Presidents enjoy getting out of Washington so much?

STRIKE UP THE BAND

Richard Nixon lets fly with his classic two-handed salute at a 1968 campaign stop in South Dakota.

HAT TRICK

Though his affable, "just folks" demeanor made
Gerald Ford a popular leader, he is the one U.S.
President who was *not* chosen by the people: he became
President after Richard Nixon resigned August 9, 1974.
When Ford ran for the office in 1976, he was rejected by
voters in a mood to clean house. Above, the incumbent
campaigns by donning the local headgear in Fresno,
California, as he trades "howdies" with the voters.

HELL-BENT FOR LEATHER

George Bush is a many-sided figure, a mix of wildly
diverse American types. He was born an East Coast
patrician, a Senator's son who attended the Phillips
Academy, Andover, and Yale. Yet his maverick decision to
seek his fortune in the Texas oil industry would make him
look right at home in cowboy boots and hat. Here he's
campaigning in a rodeo parade in Houston as Ronald
Reagan's running mate in the 1988 election.

ALA.	149,329	209,564	ILL.	800,069
ARIZ.	90,338	51,878	IND.	628,64
ARK.	35,123	48,991	IOWA	188,696
CALIF.	475,226	389,007	KAN	166,450
COLO.	102,871	64,915	KY.	353,68
CONN.	710,059	406,561	LA.	137,84
DEL.	92,328	75,16		
FLA.	512,308	361,07		
GA.	136,077	207		
IDAHO	37,971	264		

LANDSLIDE!

Dwight and Mamie Eisenhower and Richard and Pat Nixon
celebrate victory at Washington's Park Sheraton Hotel on
Election Night, November 6, 1956; they would end up
beating Adlai Stevenson and Estes Kefauver by 10 million
votes, winning 41 states to the Democrats' seven. Just prior
to going onstage—where votes were being tallied by hand—
the President indulged himself a bit. According to TIME's
original story, "... surrounded by members of his Cabinet
and other close associates, preparing to make his victory
appearance before 2,300 cheering Republicans in the hotel's
ballroom (and on the nation's television screens), Eisenhower
refused to watch Adlai Stevenson's televised concession of
defeat. He had not looked at Stevenson during the campaign,
he said, and he did not intend to start at that late hour."

"GIVE 'EM HELL, HARRY!"

Harry Truman's "whistle-stop" campaign of 1948
remains a legend in American politics. Here Truman
speaks to a crowd of Texans on October 6. From a TIME
account of his journeys: "As the 'Presidential Special' rolled
back to Washington, its cargo of frazzled newsmen were
frankly horrified at Harry Truman's endless cheerfulness and
energy. Despite a sore throat and his 64 years, he leaped out
of bed at 5 every morning, apparently unable to wait for
another exhausting day. One morning an aide caught him in
the act of taking a brisk, two-mile walk. Between breakfast
and midnight that day, Harry Truman traveled 500 miles by
train, 141 by automobile and bus, made 15 speeches in 15
different towns, changed his clothes eight times and met
250 politicians, labor leaders and civic dignitaries."

THE PEOPLE'S CHOICE

John Kennedy brought a personal magnetism to the presidency unequaled since the days of Theodore Roosevelt. Here the President is testing the surf in Santa Monica near the house of his brother-in-law, actor Peter Lawford, in August 1962. TIME reported, "When he went swimming, [people] swooned. Many of his admirers trailed after him, including one fully dressed woman. After 15 minutes, Kennedy emerged from the sea, and again he was all but mobbed."

WHOOPIN' IT UP

Bill Clinton sits in on sax with a high-school
band in Macon, Georgia, in 1992. Clinton liked to
tell students that he used to be just a fat kid playing
saxophone in the marching band—but the suggestion
that he was an outsider in his school days involved
some personal myth-making. From his earliest years,
Clinton was a bright, ambitious student; his
teachers and classmates always predicted he would
go far in public service.

THE PEOPLE'S CHOICE

THINK BIG!

The Republican Convention in Dallas in 1984 lacked suspense, for sitting President Ronald Reagan was the man of the hour. But the convention did produce this memorable image: before Reagan's pro-forma nomination and acceptance speech, Nancy Reagan addressed the faithful from the convention dais while a closed-circuit video feed showed the President watching her performance from his hotel room. When the two exchanged waves, the crowd went wild. Typically, the moment was politicized: Republicans loved its spontaneous good cheer, while Democrats had fun with the notion that it captured a truth about Reagan—his presidency, they claimed, was all larger-than-life imagery, with no substance behind the illusion.

THE PEOPLE'S CHOICE

SOUTH-BOUND

Above, President Jimmy Carter, a former Governor of Georgia, escaped the White House to receive a warm greeting from constituents in Bardstown, Kentucky, in 1979.

Left, Franklin Roosevelt frequently journeyed to Warm Springs, Georgia, to enjoy its celebrated healing waters. Here he visits with farmers en route from Atlanta to the spa in 1932. Roosevelt would die at Warm Springs in 1945.

Right, G.O.P. candidate Dwight Eisenhower and wife Mamie beam at railroad workers from their campaign train during an early-morning stop in Salisbury, North Carolina, in 1952. A male voice from the crowd shouted out, "Boy, Mamie sho' does look good, even in the mawnin'!"

Washington, 1948

Harry S Truman

He was thrust into the Oval Office by surprise—and then he surprised us with his brisk, no-nonsense character

HE WAS A VICE PRESIDENT OF THE UNITED STATES of America—but under the huge shadow of Franklin Roosevelt he did not amount to much in the minds of most Americans until that April day in 1945 when F.D.R., who seemed to go on and on, almost like a king, suddenly died. Harry Truman became the 33rd President after bursting out of Speaker Sam Rayburn's Capitol hideaway, running down a corridor and taking a wild ride through rush-hour traffic to stand in front of Eleanor Roosevelt in the White House.

"Harry, the President is dead," she said. Truman was stunned into silence. "Is there anything I can for you?" he finally asked.

"Is there anything we can do for *you?*" she replied. "For you are the one in trouble now."

Harry Truman? The forecasts of his stewardship ran the gamut from hopeless to hopeless. I was a senior in high school in the midst of a music contest on that spring day and worried about going into the Army, for war was still raging in Europe and the Pacific. "President Roosevelt died!" a friend shouted at me. There was no comprehension at first. Only shock. Then wonder. Truman was just a misty per-

sonage from faraway Washington. "Is Truman the President now?" I asked, not quite ready to believe it.

Who knew? Truman defied and contradicted most of the scholarly analysis of what makes a good or great President. He was a failed haberdasher, a sometime dirt farmer who never went to college. He had been at least a fellow traveler with Tom Pendergast, the notorious Kansas City Democratic party boss, who helped get Truman a U.S. Senate seat. Because he was not a social creature in Washington, many reporters had put him down as a rube. A competent Senator, he had earned national attention as chairman of a watchdog committee that exposed corruption and waste in the war effort, but no big bills bore his name.

Yet what lay under these public, often misleading ledger entries was something that biographer David McCullough mentioned time and time again: character. Truman believed in hard work. He was dead honest and without guile. His lack of a college degree was misleading: McCullough reckoned that the public high school education Truman received at the turn of the century from caring and gently insistent teachers was equivalent to some college degrees today. Besides, Truman was a voracious reader: his poor eyesight kept

election, Truman never lost faith in his message of caring for all the people. "He didn't just think he was going to win," said aide George Elsey, who rode the train with Truman. "He knew he would win." Character again.

Secretary of State Dean Rusk, who served under both Kennedy and Johnson, once told the story of how Truman had gone to the State Department for a meeting on the Korean War. He was briefed on military events, diplomatic progress and the economics of the conflict. Then a young aide got up to brief Truman on what was to be done politically. "Just a minute, young man," Truman snorted, jumping up out of his seat. "Stop right there. That's not your job. I take care of politics. And besides, you are not worth a damn at it anyway." Character again—seasoned with a dash of Truman's well-known vinegar.

As extravagant as he ever got was during his trips to Key West, where he wore loud sports shirts and did a rustic dog paddle in the tepid water

him from playing sports. He claimed that he had read every one of the 2,000 books—encyclopedias included—in the Independence, Missouri, library before he graduated from high school in 1901.

For decades we have asked ourselves this question: Do the huge challenges of the presidency change the nature of a man raised to the office? Or does the magnifying glass of the presidency reveal the true qualities of a man, however well concealed before? I subscribe more often than not to the latter theory. Certainly it was the case with Truman. Always he took stock, then acted forcefully, whether it was the farmer trying new techniques or the artillery captain under bombardment in World War I or the Senator investigating defense-contract fraud.

Truman never hesitated to order the dropping of atom bombs on Japan. Nor did he ever have second thoughts. His object was to save thousands of American lives that would have been lost, according to estimates, in the planned conventional invasion of Japan from the sea. History is stronger than ever now in its endorsement of Truman's tough decision.

When a host of challenging and dangerous problems emerged in the postwar years, Truman met them with courage and common sense. The Truman Doctrine, which sent aid to communist-threatened Greece and Turkey, and the Marshall Plan that followed saved war-ravaged Europe for democracy. The Berlin airlift held the Soviet Union at bay without resorting to war. When North Korea invaded South Korea, Truman did send young Americans into war. That remains a controversial initiative, but a decision most scholars think was justified.

When, against all odds, Truman won re-election over Tom Dewey in 1948, he was viewed as some kind of political wizard. He had whistle-stopped his way across America, summoning crowds from every hamlet he passed through. Though the experts all predicted defeat right up until the

The privileges of power never affected Truman, one reason why reporters loved him. He took his early-morning constitutional around the streets of Washington, and any lowly member of the press corps could tag along. Few did: it was too early and too rapid for most. He did not seek out grand resorts for recreation. He often simply went back home to Independence, sat on his screened porch, gabbed with old friends and read history and biography by the parlor lamp. In Washington he liked to cruise the Potomac River on the *Williamsburg,* the presidential yacht, play a little poker and sip some good bourbon with water. About as extravagant as he ever got on vacation was during his trips to the naval base at Key West, Florida, where he wore loud sports shirts and did a rustic dog paddle in the tepid ocean water.

Former President Jerry Ford once told me about his first encounter with Truman. Ford was a newly elected Republican Congressman from Michigan and the low man on the House public works committee. The President, tired of living in the aging, sagging White House, wanted $5 million to fix it up. He invited Ford to the executive mansion and gave him a personal tour, pointing out that there were no built-in closets, the plumbing was faulty, and his daughter Margaret's piano had poked a leg through the floor. Truman got his money—and he also got the support of Ford in many of his great foreign policy decisions.

Never did Truman in mind or heart leave ground level. When his presidency was over and he had gone back to Independence, he came out on the porch of his house for a final word with reporters who had written about him in the White House and now had seen him into retirement. What was the first thing he planned to do on his first day home? asked NBC correspondent Ray Scherer. In the same voice, with the same unadorned and sensible approach he would have used 30 years earlier, Truman replied that he was going to "carry the grips up to the attic." ■

1897

Son of Independence

c. 1901

1919

FARM BOY Truman was born on a farm in Lamar, Missouri, in 1884; his father was a successful livestock trader who moved his family to the growing city of Independence, Missouri, east of Kansas City. Harry was a fine student, but the year after he completed high school, his father went broke in the grain-futures market, ending Harry's dream of college.

TOIL After losing his money, John Truman went to work a family farm in Blue Ridge, Missouri. Harry, who had been working in Kansas City banks, quit his job and came back to help, though he liked school more than farming.

LOVE Harry and Bess Wallace met as children in Sunday school; she lived two blocks away. After he left Kansas City, he courted her by mail from the farm. When the U.S. entered World War I, Truman enlisted, even though he was 33 in 1917. The war put off their marriage until 1919; the newlyweds moved in with Bess's mother, who never quite approved of Truman.

MERCHANT After the war—he was a popular captain of artillery in France—Truman auctioned off the farm goods (his father had died in 1914) and joined with friend Eddie Jacobson to open a haberdashery in Kansas City in 1919. The store prospered at first but closed in 1922 amid a national economic slump.

c. 1920

1948

WINNER After his store failed, Truman allied himself with Kansas City's powerful Pendergast political machine and won election as a judge in Jackson County, Missouri. In 1935 he became a U.S. Senator; F.D.R. asked him to run as Vice President in 1944 after Truman chaired a committee investigating military purchasing. Despite press predictions, Truman beat Republican Tom Dewey in 1948 to remain in office.

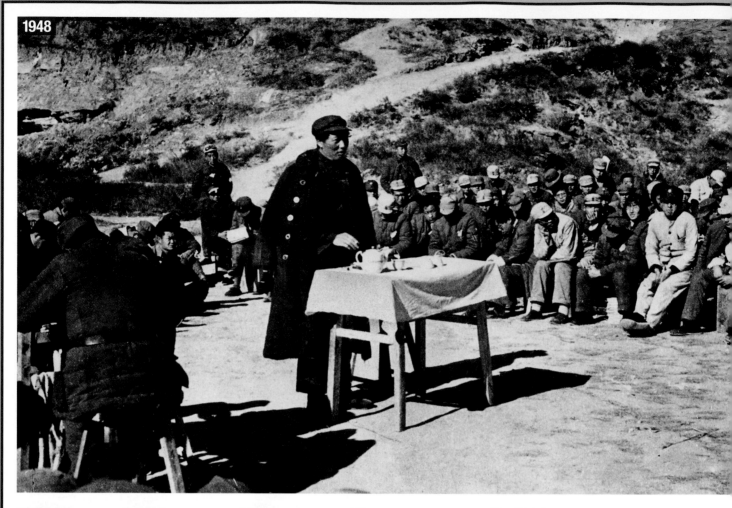

1948

The New Burdens of Power

In the critical era after World War II, Harry Truman met fresh challenges head-on

1945

1945

HOT WAR, COLD WAR: After taking the oath of office in April 1945, Truman said, "I felt the moon, the stars and all the planets had fallen on me." He faced the immense task of ending World War II and then helping build a new postwar world. Germany surrendered the month after Truman took office; in July he met with Churchill and Stalin by Potsdam, near Berlin, to discuss Germany's future and the war against Japan.

Truman was not aware of the U.S. atom bomb program until he became President, but while in Germany he ordered the dropping of the bomb on Hiroshima (survivors shown at bottom left), ending the war with Japan. He also agreed to further bomb tests at the Marshall Islands in the summer of 1946 (top center).

Occupied Berlin soon became an open sore in the new cold war. When the Russians blockaded the city, cutting it off from West Germany, Truman ordered an airlift (above) that delivered supplies. Meanwhile, Mao Zedong's armies won control of China in 1949, and North Korea invaded South Korea in 1950. Truman mustered U.N. support for a "police action" that sent 260,000 U.S. troops to war in Korea—and fired General Douglas MacArthur when he defied Truman's orders.

Reliving the Good Old Days

PLAYING AROUND Vice President Truman and Lauren Bacall teamed up to entertain servicemen early in 1945

Harry Truman's Administration was not without its scandals. And the President himself contributed to a good many controversies when he shot from the lip. But when I ran into Truman Administration graduates, I was always amazed at their loyalty to the man, through thick and thin. It was his former aide Clark Clifford who told me that Truman's own loyalty to his staff was so unshakable that they "would have died for him."

HARRY TRUMAN CALLED HIS CABINET AND STAFF together last week in Washington. There was some thunder, a great many jokes, roars of laughter and peppery irreverences about people and politics. Harry enjoyed it immensely. Well, not really. Harry was James Whitmore, the actor who plays the part in *Give 'em Hell Harry* at Ford's Theater. The National Press Club had him come for a lunch, and just to make it seem like old times they invited a lot of men and women who had worked with Truman.

There was something magic in the air. It had been 25 years since they had assembled like that. But as they lined up at the head table, the old feeling of exhilaration seized them all. Once again they felt, if only for a few moments in their imagination, that they were doing a job for a man

of purpose, courage and honor. The most eloquent moment in his Truman portrayal, said Whitmore, is the little bit where the President writes a letter to his daughter, then takes a 3¢ stamp out of his wallet and puts it on the envelope. "Very often the audience applauds," said Whitmore. "When you think about that, and I have, we have a hunger and thirst for simplicity and for people of integrity."

Clark Clifford, Truman's White House counsel, told a story of how the President dragged General Harry H. Vaughan, the controversial military aide who hated the water and boats, along on a fishing trip. When Truman caught a fish called a schoolmaster, he showed it with pride to Vaughan. "Look, Harry," said Truman, "I caught a schoolmaster." Vaughan, slumped miserably on the deck, said, "I don't give a damn if you caught a superintendent of education." When Vaughan's turn came, he recalled how he had tried to stop "all this foolishness" of Vice President Truman's playing the piano with Lauren Bacall draped languorously over its top. Of course the picture became famous.

Beth Short, Truman's correspondence secretary, contributed an anecdote about Truman's reputation for salty language. She told about the time she was on an elevator with Truman and a bunch of men. He used a swear word. "When we got to the lobby," recalled Mrs. Short, "he saw that I was on the elevator. He came over to say, 'I beg your pardon, Beth. I didn't realize you were on the elevator or I never would have said that word.'" The word was damn.

Jim Webb, who was Truman's budget man, recalled how Truman used to jump up and shake his hand every time he entered the Oval Office. Finally Webb said, "Mr. President, you don't need to do this. I've been here before." Truman said, "Oh, no. You don't know how the presidency operates. If I didn't shake hands, somebody would say, 'The President's mad at the budget director.'"

Averell Harriman, Truman's Secretary of Commerce, relived the time he had accused Ohio's Senator Robert Taft of being "the greatest friend Stalin has in the U.S." Taft had voted against the Marshall Plan and other Truman proposals. The press erupted: a particularly vehement editorial was printed in the Washington *Star.* That evening Harriman's telephone rang during dinner. "Don't pay any attention to that editorial," said Harry Truman, "because they are attacking me and not you." Declared Harriman: "That was why the President got this extraordinary loyalty from his staff. You get loyalty if you give it." And then, in a style that would have gladdened the heart of his old boss, Harriman muttered, "I still maintain that Robert Taft was Stalin's best friend in the U. S." ∎

When Politics Rode the Rails

I had as much fun writing this piece as any I have ever done. There were marvelous stories in the archives about the early days of rail campaigning. And around Washington there were a number of veterans of the great Truman train crusade of 1948. By the time I was done writing, I was hearing the whistles and feeling the clack of the wheels and imagining I was mingling with the track-side crowds and was about the only correspondent on the train advising the New York office that Harry Truman was going to win.

THE GREAT AMERICAN POLITICAL-CAMPAIGN TRAINS were like the dinosaurs. Just when they reached legendary size and importance, they were on their way to extinction, courtesy of the airplane. The greatest of all the trains ran for Harry Truman in 1948, when he clicked off 31,700 miles and delivered 356 speeches (16 in one day). Truman astonished his own political experts and the world that year by beating Republican Thomas Dewey, who was so confident of victory that he was choosing his Cabinet before any vote was cast.

"Oh, it was just great," remembers Bob Donovan, who, as a young reporter for the New York *Herald Tribune,* was with Truman the whole way. "We saw this country like never before; the wheat fields, the mountains and the little towns. Thousands and thousands of people came out and gathered around the train. It was Harry Truman's country and his kind of people. He loved it all."

Truman traveled in the ponderous and luxurious private car named *Ferdinand Magellan,* originally made for President Franklin Roosevelt. It was paneled in oak with four staterooms, bath and shower, and carried 6,000 lbs. of ice for air conditioning. The car was sheathed in steel-armor plating and 3-in. bulletproof glass. Out in the open, Truman liked the train to hit 80 m.p.h., and he would watch "our country" slide by while telling stories and sipping a little good bourbon—ready at each stop to "give 'em hell" and introduce "the boss," Bess Truman. The most famous campaign picture of all time is of a grinning Truman standing on the platform of the *Magellan* in St. Louis, holding up an early edition of the Chicago *Daily Tribune* with the headline DEWEY DEFEATS TRUMAN.

In truth, trains were used for political events from their start. But in the early days, presidential candidates did not storm the country seeking votes. William Henry Harrison actually campaigned on a train in 1836. Not until the turn of the century did modern rail campaigning begin,

with William McKinley and candidate William Jennings Bryan. Theodore Roosevelt devised the full campaign train, a rolling complex with living and office cars.

During his 12 White House years, Franklin Roosevelt set the all-time record of 243,827 miles by rail, luxuriating in America's vast beauty, campaigning, inspecting New Deal projects and, later, defense plants. Then came Truman with a political purpose and his Missouri determination. The airplane was what did in the campaign train, but television played a role—and so did the shifting U.S. population. "Trains used to come to the front door of America," says Bill Withuhn, an authority on trains at the Smithsonian. "Now they go to the backyards." Depots are shuttered; junkyards and weed patches and winos too often greet the rail traveler. Every candidate since Truman has had a train ride or two, but most of those have been nostalgic photo ops. Lady Bird Johnson led a first-ever First Lady's whistle-stop through the South for four days in 1964. There have been no follow-ups.

Stories of train campaigning grow with each retelling. A few political veterans recall Tom Dewey's blurting into an open mike when his train lurched backward that he must have "a lunatic engineer." The New York *Times*'s Scotty Reston ended his account of the incident with this line: "And then the train took off with a jerk."

HAPPY TRAILS Truman took a final ride on the *Ferdinand Magellan* when he said farewell to Washington in 1953

George Elsey, who was a young aide on Truman's great campaign trains, remembers the hard work and the sleepless nights. Once, when he took papers to Truman, who was dining with Bess, she looked up at Elsey and said, worried, "You look peaked. Have you had anything to eat?" No, admitted Elsey. "Here," she said, pushing her piece of apple pie to him, "you can eat this, and I shouldn't." The *Ferdinand Magellan* with Harry Truman rolled on into history that night, fueled by apple pie. ■

BACKSTAGE PASS

The White House is one part national museum, one part business office, one part catering hall and—to the dismay of presidential kin—one part private residence. Harry Truman called the executive mansion a "big white jail." First Families struggle to carve out a skosh of personal space here, in hopes of making the people's house … a home.

ROOM WITH A VIEW
Jimmy and Rosalynn Carter, who brought a refreshingly down-home style to the White House, put their feet up on the Truman balcony and "set a spell."

SPRING CLEANING

Jacqueline Kennedy was notably unimpressed by the White House: the Sorbonne-educated First Lady is said to have called it "that dreary Maison Blanche." With Jackie in charge (TIME called her "the cultural wagon boss of the New Frontier"), the White House was briskly de-drearied: just as she envisioned the building as a home for the arts, she believed it should be a living showplace of American craftsmanship and design. As she told Hugh Sidey for a 1961 LIFE magazine article they collaborated on: "Everything in the White House must have a reason for being there. It would be sacrilege merely to "redecorate" it—a word I hate. It must be restored—and that has nothing to do with decoration. That is a question of scholarship."

COMPANY'S COMING

Mamie Eisenhower, a hands-on mistress of the White House, inventories canned goods in the kitchen with maître d' Charles Ficklin in 1958. Mamie always took charge of the Eisenhower finances: in his 1990 book *First Ladies,* Carl Sferrazza Anthony reports that in the 1920s, when she and Ike were stationed in Washington and Mamie returned home by taxi from shopping at the military commissary, she would get out of the car at the bottom of the Connecticut Avenue hill—where the taxi zone changed and the rate increased—and carry her grocery bags up the incline to save pocket change.

BACKSTAGE PASS

BARBERSHOP CHATTER

Never one to waste a minute, Lyndon Johnson
talks politics in the barbershop in the basement
of the White House with Jack Valenti (behind
L.B.J.) and Ford Bell Sr., as Joseph Califano makes
a phone call. The barber is Steve Martini; the
manicurist is his wife. Johnson, Hugh Sidey
remembers, was quite fastidious about his appearance: his hair was always trimmed, his shoes
shined. Ironically, after Johnson left office in 1969
and returned to Texas, he let his silver hair grow
long, in the manner of the hippies and protesters
who had helped drive him from the presidency.

NIGHT MOVES

For Johnson, the presidency was a 24-hour job. Here
he receives economic aides while in bed in April 1966.
He was also known—infamously—to hold meetings
while seated on the toilet. As Sidey recalls, L.B.J. was
a "gadget man" who had placed three TVs (one per network) in the Oval Office and installed three buttons at his
chair in the Cabinet Room: when one was pushed, a waiter
would arrive bearing either Fresca, root beer or coffee. One
night when Sidey was dining privately with Johnson
upstairs at the White House, a hidden phone rang.
Without missing a bite, Johnson picked up a receiver that
had been wired to the leg of the antique dinner table.

GOLF NUTS

George Bush lines up a putt on the White House green, which was installed by the United States Golf Association shortly after Dwight Eisenhower became President. According to biographer Stephen Ambrose, Ike practiced both his approach shots and putts when he walked outside from the family quarters to the West Wing. He was furious that the White House squirrels dug holes in the green—he claimed they had been spoiled by Harry Truman, who liked to feed them. Taking Truman's view, Ronald Reagan used to gather acorns at Camp David and bring them back for the squirrels—a demonstration of enduring bipartisan support for federal squirrel subsidies.

NEXT EVENT: DOG PADDLE

Gerald Ford relaxes at the White House swimming pool in 1976 with his golden retriever, Liberty, and her pup. F.D.R. had an indoor pool put into the White House, but under Richard Nixon it was converted into the press briefing room. Ford was a devout swimmer, and an outdoor pool was built on the White House grounds after he became President. The famously clumsy Ford was soon spotted with an ugly red knob on his forehead. When Hugh Sidey and fellow reporters asked what had happened, he confessed he had bumped into the end of the new pool—"I didn't see it coming."

ROLLING THUNDER

Richard Nixon lets one fly at the bowling alley beneath the
Victorian-era Old Executive Office Building, across the street
from the White House; his average score was 180. "He may
be the most openly avid sports fan ever to occupy the White
House," Hugh Sidey noted in 1970. "In Vietnam [in 1969] this
uncomfortable man summoned up a player or a game or a team
to break the ice with the GIs he walked among."

REAL LIFE MEETS REEL LIFE

Ronald and Nancy Reagan cozy up in the snug, 47-seat
White House screening room—history does not record whether
they are watching one of the President's old efforts. Movie buff
Bill Clinton watched the 1996 blockbuster *Independence Day*
here shortly before its release. Recalling the movie's most
famous scene, producer Dean Devlin, who sat next to Clinton,
said: "Watching the White House be blown up from inside
the White House was like *The Twilight Zone*."

Whitefield, New Hampshire, 1955

Dwight D. Eisenhower

After two decades of economic depression and world war, Americans rejoiced in peace and agreed: they liked Ike

THE FIRST TIME THAT I SAW DWIGHT EISEN-hower up close and in person was in the White House Rose Garden in 1957. I was disappointed. He was not very tall or very broad. In mufti the President could have been just another of those gray-suited government bigwigs who had come to the day's ceremony in long, black limousines out of the huge gray buildings along the Mall. But he was Ike, perhaps the world's best-known and most heroic figure of the moment. What was it that made him so special?

I remembered him best from the front pages of the newspapers and the magazine spreads and the news-reels during World War II. He was in uniform in those pictures, bigger than life, surrounded by tanks and planes and acres of lean G.I.s. His battle jacket with the stars and his floppy cap and the big Eisen-hower grin were equal to an army or two. What American would not follow this man into hell?

Being President was another thing. The record of military heroes as Presidents is decidedly mixed. There was the heroic George Washington, but then there was Ulysses S. Grant, who meant well but was bur-dened with the scandals of his friends and appointees.

"Ike never had to prove himself," explained Andrew Goodpaster, a retired general and presiden-tial adviser. Eisenhower, who was already in the his-tory books, preferred to work quietly backstage ("The hidden-hand presidency," one scholar called it). Goodpaster recalled that in making his most difficult decisions, there would come a point when the Presi-dent would look around at his advisers and ask a sim-ple question: "Is it good for America?"

That may seem to be so elemental a consideration as to be laughable. But such a conclusion does not take into account the huge political forces around a President, each pressing for its own advantage, often disregarding the national interest. Indeed, as I watched Ike over the years, I began to see that people were still passionately drawn to this "average" man who stayed himself despite all temptations and who held self-serving interests at bay.

Historian Stephen Ambrose, who wrote the two-volume authorized biography of Eisenhower after reading millions of words about the man, concluded that at the center of Ike's power was trust. "I never found him in a personal lie," said Ambrose. The peo-ple who looked to Ike—Presidents, Prime Ministers, kings, dictators, generals and above all the American people—knew he told the truth.

Then there was Mamie Eisenhower's wonderful analysis of her husband's extraordinary appeal. "I'm not certain," she once said, "but I know that when I roll over in bed in the morning and feel that bald head, I'm sure the world is all right." We did that too ... well, sort of. We got a glimpse of that bald head and maybe a big Eisenhower grin and we felt better.

On that day in 1957 when I was in the Rose Garden, I caught a telling glimpse of Eisenhower in action. The event was a gathering of Medal of Honor winners from all wars. A few had had too much to drink, but they were Ike's boys. When one reached for the President's hand, he missed ... and

Ike never got careless with his immense influence and power. When the French bogged down in Vietnam and faced defeat, Ike listened to his advisers, who wanted the U.S. to jump in. He demurred. He did not say no, but he understood that this was no fight for one country to take up. Get some allies behind us and he might agree, he told his staff. None stepped up, and the idea died quietly offstage.

Ike's time in office did not meet with seamless approval. The great problems of civil rights, the inner cities and the environment began to surface, and often the President seemed preoccupied or indifferent to those concerns. Even though he did send troops to integrate a Little Rock, Arkansas, high school, he was reluctant—and, some say, tardy. These issues had never been a part of the world he had known, and his age began to show after a series of illnesses.

"That man does not deserve to be President!" Senate majority leader Lyndon Johnson once roared at me across his Capitol Hill desk. He had just come from a leadership meeting at the White House. "Old Eisenhower sits there, and I say, 'Mr. President, we've got to do something about the education bill.' And Ike looks blank and turns to one of his aides and asks, 'Do we have a bill like that?'"

L.B.J., Democrat and legislative impresario, could never understand a President who did not worry the details. There came a day in 1960, however, when Ike looked at Johnson in the Oval Office and said, "Lyndon, you ought be sitting in this chair." Presidential hopeful Johnson, suddenly awed by Ike's genius, leaked word of that sentiment with the same

When their conference following the Bay of Pigs disaster was over, the two men strolled down the walk, the neophyte President looking drawn and chastened, the hero of World War II looking relaxed and confident

fell into the rose bushes. Ike helped him up and steadied him and the grin was still in place—one soldier to another. At that moment, we all felt the man's grace.

We sometimes said that Ike had it easy being President in the years after the end of World War II. But with the passage of time, I think now that he just made it look easier than it was. The cold war was in full fury, but he edged us into the missile competition, made sure we had nuclear-powered submarines. We had a huge margin of power, and the Soviet Union knew it. Eisenhower also understood that after 20 years of depression and war, U.S. citizens needed a little time to do some things for themselves. And so new cars rolled out of the factories and backyard chefs stoked up grills for thick American steaks and Ike launched the building of the interstate highway system, giving any citizen with the itch to roam a fast road to open country.

alacrity with which he had reported his scorn for the President.

John Kennedy used to relate with some distaste an anecdote about his visit as President-elect to the White House, where he received a briefing from Eisenhower. "He didn't tell me much about foreign policy," said Kennedy. "He spent more time showing me how he could call up a helicopter to the South Lawn in a few minutes." But I recall that after the Bay of Pigs disaster, Kennedy suddenly wanted a meeting with Eisenhower up at Camp David. When it was over, the two strolled down the walk for the cameras, the neophyte President looking drawn and chastened, the World War II hero looking relaxed and confident. It was plain to see that the world was not so easy to run as Kennedy had thought it would be, and it was comforting for the nation to know that the "Old General" at his side would still answer the call to duty, a man everybody could trust. ∎

1907

KANSAS Dwight Eisenhower (center) was born on October 14, 1890, in Denison, Texas, the third of seven sons; his family moved to Abilene, Kansas, in 1891. His father, a laborer, and his mother were both Mennonite pacifists. Said Ike: "I have found out in later years we were very poor, but the glory of America is that we didn't know it then."

A Life in Uniform

1916

1932

CADET A fan of army history, Ike was a star on the West Point football team until a bad knee sidelined him. The 1915 grad met Mamie Doud, from a well-off Denver family, while on duty in Texas; they wed in 1916 and grieved when first son "Icky" died at age 3.

BRASS To his chagrin, Ike did not see action in World War I. But he moved up in the Army, with postings in Washington and Paris; he served four years under George Marshall and 10 under Douglas MacArthur (left), who became a role model. From 1935 to 1939, Eisenhower worked under MacArthur as assistant military adviser to the Philippine government.

HERO Eisenhower returned to the U.S. in 1939, just as World War II began. After Pearl Harbor, Army Chief of Staff Marshall put Ike in charge of defending the Philippines, then of the 1942 invasion of Africa and finally of the 1944 D-day invasion. At left, Ike and Generals George Patton (far left) and Omar Bradley look on in 1945 as concentration-camp survivors show how they were tortured.

1945

1955

PRESIDENT Truman asked Ike to be his running mate in 1948, but Ike refused. Putting aside his initial reluctance to be the Republican candidate in 1952, he easily beat Adlai Stevenson in the race. Taking office at age 62, Ike suffered a heart attack in 1955 (left) and a mild stroke in 1957.

1959

1956

An Age of Atomic Anxiety

Dwight Eisenhower faced a cold war abroad and McCarthyism and racial strife at home

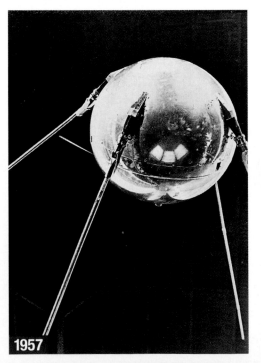

1957

1954

1960

1957

ADVERSARIES: Dwight D. Eisenhower faced the new challenges of cold war in an atomic age. The Korean War ended in a stalemate, but the Soviets tightened their grip over Eastern Europe, sending tanks into Hungary in 1956 to crush a revolt. The Soviets took the cold war into a new sphere in 1957, launching the satellite Sputnik to beat the U.S. into space. When the charismatic rebel Fidel Castro seized power in Cuba in 1959, he brought a whiff of revolution close to U.S. soil. Ike suffered a setback in 1960: when the Soviets shot down a U.S. U-2 spy plane (above), he initially denied knowledge of such flights, handing blustering Soviet leader Nikita Khrushchev a major propaganda victory.

At home, Eisenhower faced a "red scare" fostered by Senator Joseph McCarthy (below left) and others, but he did not denounce McCarthy, and the Senator lost many of his followers after the Army-McCarthy hearings of 1954. As U.S. blacks began to demand equal rights, the President reluctantly sent federal troops to Little Rock, Arkansas, to ensure the peaceful integration of Central High School.

The Powerful Smile of Sincerity

AILING Eisenhower spoke to Republicans in Miami Beach from Walter Reed Hospital; he suffered a heart attack the next day

Dwight Eisenhower, the military man, was not chummy with reporters. There were none of those intimate chats backstage that I had with other Presidents whom I had covered in political campaigns. But I saw Ike in the Rose Garden at formal speeches and at press conferences, where we were not allowed to have tape recorders but had to rely on pencils and pads. This LIFE column was written seven years after Ike left office: in a crisis-ridden summer, Ike had risen from a sickbed to make a video address to the Republican Convention. Ike was, in his personal deportment at least, a man from another age. Still, I confess that like most of America, I had a great affection for this general/President. I guess I had some of the feeling of Mamie: when I saw Ike's bald head and his grin, I felt the country was in good hands.

FORMER PRESIDENT DWIGHT EISENHOWER CAME into the living rooms of 30 million Americans the other night, and he was old and bald and he used a TelePrompTer and he still flubbed a few of his lines, but there was more power in his 10-minute appeal than in any of the presidential political oratory of the past 12 months. And it may be that the effort to make his talk

brought on the heart attack that has left him seriously ill.

It has been one of those mysteries of national life why all the would-be Presidents (and President Johnson) who have been frantically searching for some formula to catapult them to the heights of popularity have failed to study the example of Eisenhower. Perhaps in this age of contrivance the formula is too simple to be believed—decency, sincerity and honesty. They shine out of Ike like a beacon, and it should give those in the political business some pause. Because they illustrate anew that all the programs espoused and the bills passed and the billions spent are only a part of this thing of being President, and maybe even the lesser part in a time of dispirited affluence.

It should be of some significance that while almost everybody else was engaged in a season of shifting views, cloaked opinions, denials of internal trouble and even espousal of the right of a government to lie to its people, the steady virtue of Eisenhower raised him to a new pedestal while all those others fell lower. He was polled the most admired man in the nation last year and probably ranks as high today. There is some kind of hunger there. Even among the unwashed and on the campus, the cry is for candor and compassion, which is the same thing.

Lyndon Johnson has used an inordinate amount of his

time and energy raising monuments to his own greatness, and all the while his esteem has slipped. Eisenhower's self-promotion runs at such a low voltage as to be indiscernible. He still acts a little embarrassed at new honors. He still wonders why people care—and that only intensifies the phenomenon. A while back in his modest office on the corner of the Gettysburg College campus, he marveled at this public. He didn't have an unusually big nose or extraordinary ears or any other physical features that made him easily identifiable, he explained. Yet, there he had been in New York City in the back of an unmarked limousine, almost out of sight, and as he drove down the street, "the darnedest thing happened. People leaned out and yelled, 'Hello, Ike.' How did they know who I was?"

While all the candidates from Reagan to McCarthy diagnosed in detail the national ailments, Ike maintained a hearty belief that it was a fever, and the body was fundamentally sound. He could beat any of them in a runoff. While the scowl has become the symbol of this season's stump (with the exception of Hubert Humphrey), there has been that enduring smile of Eisenhower's that reached more men's hearts than Social Security. There is the feeling from Ike that he trusts people and they return it in spades. He has confessed that it would be nice sometime to take Mamie and go to the Metropolitan Museum and "just drift through it without having to shake hands or sign an autograph." But, says Ike, with a chuckle, whenever he brings up that complaint (one of the few anybody has heard him make about his lot in life), Mamie turns to him and says, "How would you like it if they all disliked you?"

In these days of rebellion against order, Ike has been more than ever conscious of the example he must set, which is another of those unmeasurable qualities that go into leadership and has been missing on occasion with the men now in the ring. Eisenhower confesses a liking for horses and horse racing, and yet he has scrupulously limited himself to one appearance at the track each year, simply because he believes that that is enough for a man who is held in the public gaze.

There are a lot of people who still feel that Ike never really understood his job of being President. Yet today his common-sense observations about the presidency are more cogent than a lot of the other talk. He, for instance, does not like the disuse of the Cabinet and the National Security Council in the Executive Branch, and the resulting deep personalization of the presidency. "You need," he says, "bitterly debated advice and conflicting con-

siderations." The frantic pace of today's presidency has also disturbed him. He played golf, yes, but the business was never out of his mind. "A President has got to have time to think about his main problems." There are a growing number of presidential observers who endorse that need.

He feels that the heads of the great federal departments should have more far-reaching power in setting up their staffs. He feels that the momentum of the big bureaucracies tends to sweep the Cabinet officers right along with them, and these men are often almost powerless to combat the system, which grows bigger when it is obvious that in some ways it should grow smaller. This is the theme song now of all the candidates.

So far American historians have not ranked Eisenhower very high in the presidential legend. But there is growing conviction that the measure of the man himself may have been more of a factor in the national life than anyone has been willing to admit before. Ike has not been referred to as a top-drawer expediter, one who knew the machinery of government, but there are hints that the traditional assessment of those qualities may be outdated and inaccurate. The eight years of relative world calm under Ike, achieved without losing any territory or much prestige, have taken on new importance. There are even those who dare suggest that his soothing spirit, the innate goodness of the man himself, did more to lift up the hearts of Americans and hold them together in a reasonable state of public happiness than many of the social reforms that have been propounded since. ■

BITTER SUMMER Only weeks after Ike's speech to the G.O.P. Convention, cops busted protesters' heads at the Democratic Convention in Chicago

THE CHILDREN'S HOUR

John and Caroline Kennedy add
a rare quality—joy—to the Oval
Office, more often a crucible of crisis.

INNER CIRCLE

According to Richard Nixon, life in the
White House fishbowl presents a "paradoxical
combination of loss of privacy and sense of
isolation." As Presidents struggle to keep a sense of proportion
while everyone around them is busily hailing the chief, they reach
out to their families for support, perspective—and laughter.

SUNSET

In the last few days of his presidency, Jimmy Carter negotiated feverishly with Iran over the release of the Americans held hostage in Tehran for 14 months. The Iranians refused to release the prisoners until Ronald Reagan was sworn in. Here, hours after Reagan's Inauguration, Jimmy and Rosalynn comfort daughter Amy, who was upset at leaving Washington in the middle of the school year to return to Georgia. Said Carter: "Come on, everybody. This is a time to be happy. Get on board." Six school friends flew with Amy to see her home, returning with the jet to Washington that night.

SUNRISE

In 1946 World War II veteran Richard Nixon, 33, was elected to the House of Representatives from California's 12th District. Here Nixon, wife Pat and 13-month-old Tricia take in the cherry blossoms along the capital's Tidal Basin in the spring of 1947. (Daughter Julie would be born in 1948.) Nixon soon met another first-term Representative, John F. Kennedy; they both served on the House Education and Labor Committee. Returning by train one night from a debate in Pennsylvania— their first—they shared a sleeper and drew straws for the lower berth. Nixon won.

RISE AND SHINE

George and Barbara Bush enjoy the company of their grandchildren, as shown in this 1987 picture, taken at the couple's home in Kennebunkport, Maine, when Bush was Vice President. The picture was snapped by David Valdez, who served for nine years as official photographer for the Bushes (or, as the President called him in his unique parlance, "a photo dog"). The woman seated at right is Margaret Bush, wife of the Bushes' son Marvin. From left, the Bush grandchildren are: Pierce (son of Neil and Sharon Bush), twins Barbara and Jenna (daughters of George W. and Laura Bush) in bed, Marshall (daughter of Margaret and Marvin Bush), Jeb Jr. (son of Jeb and Columba Bush) and Sam LeBlond (son of Dorothy Bush and her first husband, William LeBlond).

SKIRTING THE ISSUE

From the White House to your house, some moments are universal. At Bill Clinton's second Inauguration, daughter Chelsea, 16, dazzled the crowd—and here she shows her mother why. TIME's report: "Along much of the length of the Inauguration parade, Chelsea Clinton had gone coatless, displaying a blue-gray jacket and a matching skirt with the kind of hemline that makes headlines—the better to show off her ballroom-ready legs. Back at the White House, she gave her mother a proud reprise of her fashion statement."

HEY, GOOD-LOOKIN'

It was a storybook romance: once upon a time, the
President's eight-year-old grandson caught the eye of
the Vice President's eight-year-old daughter ... and
nature took its course. David Eisenhower and Julie
Nixon met on the ceremonial platform at Dwight
Eisenhower's second Inauguration, in 1957—a location
not generally regarded as a lover's lane. They married
on December 22, 1968, just before Nixon took office;
Julie wore the thin blue garter saved by Mamie Doud
from her wedding to Dwight Eisenhower in 1916.

WEDDING BELLES

Facing page, Julie and Tricia Nixon enjoy a sisterly moment before Tricia's wedding to New York City lawyer Ed Cox. The ceremony was held in the White House Rose Garden in June 1971. "Tricia's wedding was a glorious day at the White House," Hugh Sidey recalls. "Richard Nixon could be so good at times. The sinister mantle would be shed, and he could be gracious and elegant. His daughters never deserted him, through all the dark days of Watergate. They are two of the finest children to emerge from the White House— and I think Pat Nixon should get a lot of the credit for their strong character."

FATHER OF THE BRIDE

Relegated to supporting roles at daughter Luci's wedding to Patrick Nugent in 1966, Lyndon and Lady Bird Johnson look as if they're more than ready for the ceremony to start, above. If L.B.J. seems especially grumpy, it may be because there is no telephone in the vicinity. He perked up later, at left, when he escorted Luci down the aisle.

Discussing growing up in the White House, Luci told LIFE magazine, "Warren G. Harding ran for President on a platform of 'a return to normalcy.' I don't believe there is anything that approaches 'normalcy' for a First Family—or anything a First Family's children crave more."

AND FALA MAKES THREE

The Roosevelts raised a family of five, but by the time F.D.R. became President, their children had grown. Although a couple of grandchildren sometimes resided in the White House, the Roosevelts ran the establishment for adults: the cocktail hour was a daily ritual. In the absence of White House children, it was F.D.R.'s Scotch terrier, Fala, that captured the fancy of the nation. A 1940 gift from the President's cousin, Fala is seen here with the Roosevelts on the veranda of their home in Hyde Park, New York, in 1941. And yes, that is proto-feminist Eleanor Roosevelt—knitting.

FILLING IN

Two months after Gerald Ford became President, his wife Betty underwent a mastectomy (which she bravely refused to keep secret). Their daughter Susan, 17, gamely agreed to fill in for her mother as host at a diplomatic reception. Recalling the occasion for LIFE magazine in 1992, Susan wrote, "I was not prepared to be the unofficial First Lady. My father and I were in the Yellow Oval Room [in the family quarters of the White House] waiting to be escorted downstairs. I had never worn long white gloves before. And I was scared to death that I might do something wrong … For a teenager, the White House seemed like a cross between a reform school and a convent."

Onboard the *Honey Fitz*
off Hyannis Port,
Massachusetts, 1963

John Fitzgerald Kennedy

Radiating promise, he beckoned us to a New Frontier and faced down Khrushchev, but fate denied him fulfillment

SO MANY THINGS CAME TOGETHER FOR JOHN Kennedy. He was a scion of wealth beyond belief, a member of a large self-promoting family of power and prominence; he was intelligent, handsome and athletic (to the extent a bad back would allow); he was a genuine war hero and a serious student of world affairs; he had a glamorous wife and children, a pleasing manner, a strong stage presence—and he found a world that was waiting for such a leader.

"Life is unfair," he said, and the grace of that statement was that he understood he had been given more than his share. He would try to make up for it to others through politics, good Democrat that he was. But in private, he was not a particularly generous man. He was going to enjoy what he had to the fullest. And he did. His idea was that there was plenty more to go around, and after all, his father, Ambassador Joseph Kennedy, had a right to his fortune since he had earned it—or, some said, stolen it. But then in the roaring years when Old Joe got his many millions, a lot of others did the same, and probably none of them could survive a rigorous honesty test.

Kennedy turned his humor on the situation. Cam-paigning in Wisconsin in 1960, he asked me to have lunch with him at an airport lunch counter. The meal finished, he felt in his pockets. All empty. He gave me a forlorn look and asked if I would pay. I paid the bill but left no tip. Back then, who ever left a tip at a counter? "Leave a tip," he ordered. So I did. Kennedy leaned over, meticulously counted each coin, looked back at me (this time with that big grin) and said, "Pretty chintzy. Leave some more." So I did.

Then one day he was President—barely—but President. We had a great blizzard the night before his Inauguration, and I never did get to sleep. The next morning I battled my way through the snow drifts and finally to the White House, where I joined the motorcade to the Capitol steps for the ceremony. I stood on the pedestal of one of the columns behind the new President and heard those words echo over the plaza: "Ask not what your country can do for you—ask what you can do for your country." I was no longer weary, nor were the thousands of onlookers standing in the snow. There was new energy, a new view on the far horizon that I suspected was felt all over America.

But the world soon got ugly. There was the disaster

of the Bay of Pigs, when Kennedy would not use American forces to help the invaders, who foundered and were killed or captured. The Soviet Union began to squeeze West Berlin, the island of freedom within satellite East Germany. Communist forces marched in Southeast Asia. Kennedy flew to Vienna for a summit with Soviet boss Nikita Khrushchev, who pounded the table and declared that Berlin was a bone stuck in his throat and it must come out.

When the summit was over, Kennedy went to Palm Beach, Florida, to lick his wounds and ponder the future of the free world. I had dinner with him in one of the grand beach mansions, much of the furniture shrouded in dust covers because it was late June, long after the winter season. We talked of the possibility of nuclear war, of troubles in Southeast Asia, while Frank Sinatra records played in the background and we

somebody uses them. I think it is going to be the same with nuclear weapons."

But Kennedy never showed that side of himself to the public. Under Jacqueline Kennedy's graceful and artistic touch, the White House was more beautiful than it had ever been. The dinners for Nobel Prize winners and for André Malraux, France's Minister of Culture, were stunningly innovative ensembles of decoration, guests and entertainment. Pablo Casals, the world's leading cellist, came back to the White House to play for American composers and musicians, and the glamour mounted, though Mrs. Kennedy whispered to a friend, "The only music [the President] really appreciates is *Hail to the Chief.*"

Was there a Camelot? The idea is much derided by Kennedy critics, who were and are legion. Maybe the label is a little strong, but there was a special feeling in those years when young men and women who had served in war and now sought a lasting peace and a just society came to Washington under the banner of the New Frontier. Yes, there was a dark side, known to those of us who followed Kennedy closely. He was a careless womanizer, but the world moved fast, and we never saw his philandering interfere with his presidency. Nor were there confessions, diaries, tapes or recorded phone calls to prove what seemed so clear from circumstantial evidence. Yet this was a deeply disappointing failure of character.

Once when I went in to see Kennedy, he had a frown on his face from a misbehaving world. "I'm going to give this damned job to Nixon," he snorted, then looked at me with a bemused expression. He relished the job. He saw himself out on a stage with the historic figures of Churchill, De Gaulle and Roosevelt. "I love the chess game of power," he said. In danger there was exhilaration, and I saw it in his face from down below when he shouted *"Ich bin ein Berliner!"* to a huge crowd. The impact of the roar that followed was almost physical.

Kennedy confronted racial discrimination in Alabama and

J.F.K. was moving toward the high ground of world leadership when he went to Dallas. I rode in the first press bus, laughing in the sunshine ...

sipped daiquiris on a patio in the soft summer evening. Strange, rushing world, surreal world, here surrounded by opulence and Frank, nasty communists so far away.

"I've never met a man like that," Kennedy said, recounting the discussions in Vienna with Khrushchev. "Up until now when there has been a problem that hurt everyone, if it was not resolved, I could always find a way to work something out. When I brought up the fact that if we let things get out of control and there was a nuclear exchange, 70 million people would die within 10 minutes, Khrushchev seemed not to care. He just looked at me."

All through that summer of 1961, as the Berlin Wall went up and the threats in Southeast Asia grew, Kennedy moved in and out of anxiety. One evening when I went into the Oval Office, he was deeply pessimistic. "If I read history correctly," he said, "when a new weapon is invented—going all the way back to the longbow—they build up and build up, then

Mississippi. The Peace Corps soared. A war on poverty was put into planning. In the Cuban missile crisis, Kennedy stared down his old adversary Khrushchev and brought a peaceful solution to a frightening challenge. That established J.F.K.'s toughness, and then he held out a hand of cooperation to the Soviets in his famous speech at American University, when he praised the Russian people for their many achievements and urged both Americans and citizens of the Soviet Union to direct their attention to common interests.

Kennedy was moving toward the high ground of world leadership when he went to Dallas late in 1963. I rode in the first press bus 50 yards behind the President, and I laughed in the sunshine at the brazen electioneering and the joy of the whole wide-open Texas day, and then as we turned a corner and headed for a strange, ugly building at the end of the street, I heard the three sharp explosions that changed America and the world. ■

1925

1948

1946

Fortunate Son

1960

1963

AFFLUENCE John Kennedy was born into one of America's wealthiest families on May 29, 1917, the second son of nine children. His father Joseph earned millions in banking, the stock market and as a Hollywood producer. Politics was in J.F.K.'s blood: his mother Rose Fitzgerald was the daughter of a mayor of Boston. Of Irish-immigrant stock, J.F.K. would become the first Roman Catholic President of the U.S.

THE CLAN Franklin Roosevelt named Joe Kennedy U.S. ambassador to England late in 1937; an isolationist, Joe opposed U.S. entry into the war. The next years brought tragedy for the family: eldest son Joe Jr. was killed in action in 1944; eldest daughter Kathleen died in an air crash in 1948; John almost died in the South Pacific. The family gathered after the war: from left, John, Jean, Rose, Joe, Pat, Bobby, Eunice, Teddy (front). Missing is mentally retarded sister Rosemary.

CANDIDATE J.F.K. picked up the baton from his fallen elder brother, whom Joe Sr. had groomed for office. The handsome war hero and Harvard graduate was easily elected to represent the Bay State's 11th District in 1946.

BROTHERS Elected to the Senate in 1952, J.F.K. was re-elected in 1958. As President, he surprised many by naming brother Bobby, his top aide, as Attorney General. When Teddy won the election to fill J.F.K.'s Senate seat in 1962, it was clear America had a new political dynasty on its hands.

FAMILY TIME Kennedy's much-touted charisma was the product of his wealth, his good looks, his heroism in war—and of his chic wife Jacqueline Bouvier, herself the daughter of a wealthy Eastern family. They met in 1951 and married in 1953. Daughter Caroline was born in 1957, son John Jr. in 1960. A second son, Patrick, died two days after birth in 1963.

1961

High Noon of the Cold War

From Cuba to Berlin to space, John Kennedy squared off against Nikita Khrushchev

1961

1961

CHERRY PICKER

LAUNCH PAD WITH ERECTOR

LAUNCH PAD WITH ERECTOR

MISSILE READY BLDGS

CABLING

FUELING VEHICLES

1962

1961

1962

1,000 DAYS: In his brief time in office—less than three years—John Kennedy faced a rash of crises abroad, as the grandstanding Soviet leader Nikita Khrushchev pushed to find the young President's pressure points. Kennedy's term began with the dismal fiasco at the Bay of Pigs in Cuba, when a ragtag band of U.S.-backed invaders were trounced by Fidel Castro's troops (bottom left). That August, following a June summit meeting in Vienna, the Soviets' proxy government in East Germany began putting up the Berlin Wall (above), the paramount symbol of the cold war.

In October 1962, the tension crested when U.S. spy planes found Soviet-built missiles being installed in Cuba, close to U.S. shores (top center). J.F.K. demanded their removal, and after a week of high-wire negotiations, the Soviets backed down. Across the globe, J.F.K. sent a small number of U.S. advisers to Vietnam (left), as communist guerrillas under Ho Chi Minh threatened South Vietnam's pro-Western government. With the space race heating up, J.F.K. vowed to pass the Russians and hailed astronaut John Glenn's orbit of the earth—even though Glenn followed a path blazed by the U.S.S.R.'s Yuri Gagarin.

At home, the civil rights movement gathered steam, as Freedom Riders boarded buses to help integrate Southern transit and other public facilities (top left). Kennedy sent federal troops to ensure the safety of James Meredith, the first black to attend the University of Mississippi.

What the Ks Really Said

The interview with Kennedy after the Vienna summit with Nikita Khrushchev was one of those surreal experiences that journalists sometimes encounter in pursuit of powerful people. Vienna had been out from under the Soviet thumb only a few years, and it was still a gray, rather grim city; troops walked in its streets and police dogs patrolled sensitive spots. The President's party had jetted from there to Palm Beach, one of the most indulgent cultures in the world. Kennedy made the transition effortlessly, looking all the while as we talked like an aristocratic beach boy. But I could not shake the last glimpse I had of him in Vienna: instead of the usual smile, he gave me a grim look, brow furrowed, and his fingers drummed nervously. It would be a long, tense summer.

SUMMIT When Kennedy dropped a match, Khrushchev laughed and called him "a capitalist, not an incendiary"

PRESIDENT KENNEDY LAST WEEKEND THOUGHT back over his talks with Khrushchev. "The next 10 years," he said, "are going to be difficult. I came away feeling that in view of the Russian commitment to our system in the same areas, it was going to be a close thing to prevent war. There is heightened danger for both countries." The bland communiqué released from Vienna told little of the drama that actually took place in meetings that began pleasantly—but ended in an exchange of grim warnings. What follows is what happened:

When the two leaders sat down in the music room of the U.S. embassy residence, the President told the Premier that he had met him during his visit to the U.S. two years ago and was glad to see him again. Khrushchev answered in the same tone: he had had his eye on Kennedy for some time as an up-and-coming politician. Then they got down to work. Khrushchev did not indulge in any of his familiar buffoonery. Like Kennedy, he had obviously prepared carefully for the talks. He quoted excerpts from the speech Kennedy had made to Congress the week before, then added, "I've read all your speeches." He had also read U.S. newspapers. Once he declared that Kennedy had reversed an order to send U.S. Marines into Laos; when J.F.K. denied it, Khrushchev shot him an unbelieving look and said he had read it in the American press.

At one point Khrushchev dryly noted that Western powers had interfered in Russia's 1917 revolution, and he maintained that the U.S. was still opposing wars of liberation—"holy wars," he called them, wars that were "the desire of the people." The tide of history, he insisted, is with communism. "You're an old country; we're a young country," he said. Kennedy had an answer: "If you'll look across the table," he said, "you'll see that we're not so old."

When Kennedy quoted two Chinese proverbs, Khrushchev gave him an amused look and said, "You seem to know the Chinese very well." "We may *both* get to know them better," Kennedy answered. Khrushchev said seriously, "I know them well now." As for Cuba, Khrushchev did not challenge Kennedy on the recent Bay of Pigs invasion fiasco, but he expressed admiration for Castro and said that the U.S. was fast making Castro a good communist. Kennedy bluntly denied it.

But it was only at the end of the meetings that the basic disagreements between the U.S. and Russia flared into open bitterness. The subject was Berlin. Both men stated their stands. Then, as they argued back and forth, neither able to budge the other, Khrushchev's temper kindled and Kennedy grew even sterner. No possible area of agreement could be found. At the final lunch Kennedy gestured toward a model of the U.S. warship *Constitution* sitting on the table and said that Old Ironsides' guns carried only half a mile. In those days it had been possible for nations to recover from war, as indeed Western Europe had done after World War II. But today a war would go through generations of men. On this note of warning the talks ended.

Kennedy and his U.S. team were not "shocked" by Khrushchev, as has been reported. The real-life Khrushchev was even tougher than they had imagined, but they are sure that he was impressed by J.F.K.'s own knowledge and toughness. Perhaps most important of all, the President has decided that the U.S. must step up its contingency planning on Berlin and be ready for anything. ■

Memories of John F. Kennedy

I stretched things a bit in this column. Actually the small, human routines of Kennedy were quite normal. But when a millionaire, a war hero, a President, the most powerful man on earth does such things they become rather unusual. I did not include my favorite Kennedy moment in this column, written 10 years after his death: one day when I walked into the Oval Office for an interview, he said, "Hugh, let's get out of here. Let's go for a swim." I protested I had never thought about bringing a swimming suit to a presidential interview. "You don't need one in this pool," he replied, leading the way to the indoor pool that Franklin Roosevelt had installed. Kennedy stripped down. So did I. We plunged in naked, and I conducted the only aquatic interview of my career.

THE ONCE-OVER Kennedy surveys the 1959 Rice Queen

NOTHING IS QUITE SO MEMORABLE ABOUT JOHN Kennedy as his normality. When he saw a pretty girl, he surveyed her expertly and sometimes invoked presidential political privilege and shook hands, lingering a moment or two for close inspection. "I never cared much for El Morocco and nightclub life," he said about his salad days. "Just give me a beach and a girl anytime." After he had called the Big Steel executives s.o.b.'s in 1962, he was asked how come he had violated his own rule against indulgence in anger. "Because it felt so good," he said, grinning.

Out at Lassen Volcanic National Park in California, he became fascinated with the deer that came to his cabin for a handout. He kept calling for more food to feed them on this rare wilderness excursion. The next morning his eggs came without toast. "You fed all the bread to the deer," the chagrined President was told. One morning Dean Rusk got an angry phone call from Kennedy complaining about a news leak. Find the culprit, barked Kennedy. Rusk went to unusual lengths to trace the leak, finally called in the reporter himself for a grilling. The Secretary of State called J.F.K. back. "I've found the leak," he told Kennedy. "It's you. Yesterday in your office at 4 p.m."

When the brothers J.F.K. and R.F.K. were noted among the better-dressed males of the nation, John Kennedy complained with a great smile, "I understand how I made it. I'm pretty well dressed. But Bobby isn't." After the Inauguration, when he was told that Clare Boothe Luce had said that Teddy Kennedy "looked like a Greek god," J.F.K. said with a delightfully wicked grin, "Are you sure she didn't say he looked like a goddam Greek?"

And when a piece came out saying that Attorney General Robert Kennedy was the second most powerful man in the world, the President picked up his phone in the presence of a visitor, listened a few seconds, then turned from the receiver to announce, "This is the second most powerful man in the world on the line." Turning back, Kennedy listened again, then started to laugh. "Bobby wants to know who is No. 1."

In the midst of high affairs of state, military aide Chester V. (Ted) Clifton used to get a special signal. He knew what to do. He squared his shoulders, marched out of the room, returned with an important-looking folder, put it discreetly in J.F.K.'s hand. Inside was a cigar.

Down at the ranch of Oklahoma's Senator Bob Kerr, Kennedy kept ignoring Kerr's prize bulls on display and asking about the cowboys who herded them in front of him. "How much do cowboys make a week? Where do they live? How come they get free electricity and free milk?" As an author, J.F.K. had some sound advice for new writers. "Don't send out many free books. Tell your friends that if they really are friends they will buy the book." Once when he was driving down New York City's Fifth Avenue, he leaned forward in his seat as he passed St. Patrick's Cathedral. He gave a little wave and a salute and with a chuckle said, "Thanks for everything."

Kennedy came off his plane at Newport, Rhode Island, one bright day in the middle of his presidency. He stood in the wind as the Navy band played *Hail to the Chief.* Walking by a group of reporters, he said, "Don't you love the beat of that piece?" He strode off laughing, pleased with himself and his job. ∎

SOUL MATES
Lyndon Johnson and his good friend Yuki get in touch with their inner wolves in 1968.

AT EASE

"If you can't stand the heat, get out of the kitchen," Harry Truman declared. There are other ways to escape the high temperature in the Oval Office: F.D.R. often ended the day with his stamp collection, while Truman often began the day with a brisk walk. L.B.J. and Reagan were horsemen; Ike played golf and Nixon played piano. And when all else fails, a President can always summon a buddy and howl at the moon.

ROUGHING IT

Immediately after winning the Republican nomination for the presidency at the 1952 convention in Chicago, Dwight Eisenhower vacationed at his friend Aksel Nielsen's ranch in Fraser, Colorado. Here, Ike handles morning K.P. duty. He also indulged another hobby: painting. Mamie Doud Eisenhower had grown up in Denver, and Ike loved Colorado; Cherry Hills was his favorite golf course, and he kept a small office at Lowry Air Force Base for use during summer vacations.

GONE FISHIN'

Harry Truman—bow tie and all—plainly relishes a day spent angling on Puget Sound with Washington State Governor Mon Wallgreen, second from right, in 1945. Truman was not a great outdoorsman, but he was the nation's foremost proponent of the morning constitutional, which he conducted at a brisk pace. He did not own a "summer White House": he preferred to spend vacations at his home in Independence, Missouri, or, in wintertime, at the U.S. naval base in Key West, Florida.

NO PAIN, NO GAIN

Left, Harry Truman returns from a 1947 trip to South America on the U.S.S. *Missouri*. TIME's report: "No devotee of calisthenics, the President nevertheless acquiesced when restive newsmen formed the Truman Athletic Club and asked him to lead them in a round of light exercise. Coach Truman wore a T.A.C. T-shirt and a harness racer's cap, one of many special pieces of headgear he sported at sea."

PLAY IT AGAIN, BILL

Right, TIME photographer P.F. Bentley shadowed Bill Clinton during his first campaign for the White House. Here, on a hotel balcony in Los Angeles, the candidate is limbering up on his saxophone for an appearance on *The Arsenio Hall Show*.

ANCHORS AWEIGH

Left, John F. Kennedy, an ardent sailor from his early years, takes the wheel of a sailboat in 1960. Family wealth allowed J.F.K. to enjoy several getaways from the White House, including vacation homes at both Hyannis Port, Massachusetts, and Palm Beach, Florida.

FARMER IN CHIEF

Jimmy Carter walks through the fields of his family farm in Plains, Georgia, in February 1976, just before embarking on a grueling series of primaries that ultimately brought him the Democratic presidential nomination. TIME ran this picture in May of that year, after Carter had emerged as the clear front runner, in a cover story titled "Jimmy's Breakthrough."

This picture captures a key aspect of Carter's personality: his penchant for privacy. As TIME's story noted, "There may be something unknowable about him, an inner man that has not been—and may never be—revealed ... Though he speaks almost mystically of the 'intense friendships' that he has formed with Americans almost everywhere, Carter has few cronies, and he keeps even them at arm's length. He shares his most intimate thoughts and feelings with only one person—his wife Rosalynn. Says Gerald Rafshoon, an Atlanta friend who handles Carter's campaign advertising: 'You don't get that close to Jimmy, because he retreats.'"

WALK SOFTLY

Above, Dwight Eisenhower enjoys a quail hunt at the Georgia plantation of his first Secretary of the Treasury, George Humphrey, just after leaving the presidency, in 1961. Readers of Tom Wolfe's 1998 novel, *A Man in Full,* will note the trappings of such outings haven't changed.

HEAD 'EM UP!

Left, Lyndon Johnson rides tall in the saddle as he puts his horse, Lady B., through her paces on the L.B.J. Ranch, his spread near Stonewall, Texas. Hubert Humphrey observed: "Rest for him was controlled frenzy." TIME got on L.B.J.'s bad side by publishing a 1964 account of his driving a Lincoln Continental at 90 m.p.h. along the backroads of the ranch while drinking beer from a paper cup.

CLEAN-UP TIME

Right, Ronald Reagan does a horseman's chores during a 1988 visit to his 688-acre Rancho del Cielo near Santa Barbara, California. The lifelong rider would later write in his autobiography, "how much of the experience is physical and how much is mental, I don't know, but there's no better place for me to think than on top of a horse."

THE MUSIC MAN

Richard Nixon, an accomplished pianist, practices
Deep in the Heart of Texas before a visit to the L.B.J. Ranch
in August 1968, shortly after he won the G.O.P. presidential nomination. Nixon loved classical music—he claimed
his two great unfulfilled ambitions were to conduct a
symphony orchestra and play an organ in a cathedral. His
aunt was a gifted player and teacher; when Richard was 12
and showed promise on the piano, he left his family for six
months to live with her and take daily lessons.

FOILED AGAIN

What duffer doesn't recognize this expression? Certainly
the President gave the ball a firm stroke—no doubt it was
his putter that betrayed him. An exuberant—if erratic—
golfer, Gerald Ford became more famous for beaning
bystanders than for smiting the sphere; here he's playing in
the Lee Elder Tournament at Lake of the Woods Country
Club in Virginia in 1975. Ford likes to recount the joke
Bob Hope often told on him: "The President hit two
bogeys, two double bogeys and two spectators."

L.B.J. Ranch, Texas, 1967

Lyndon Baines Johnson

He nurtured dreams as big as the Texas sky, but in the end he found all his tall tales couldn't change reality

LYNDON B. JOHNSON WAS THE SINGLE MOST fascinating man that I have ever met. He was majority leader of the U.S. Senate when I went up to the Capitol for my first foray into his territory, which he ruled like a proud lion. He met me in a shadowy corridor outside the Senate Gallery, clapped my hesitant shoulders between his big hands and, looking down his nose at me, said, "I never knew a reporter who didn't have a character flaw. What's yours?" I was speechless, which he had anticipated. My character flaw.

Then there was the day when he spent three hours telling me why he would never agree to accept a vice-presidential nomination under John Kennedy. J.F.K. heard I'd been in with Johnson and summoned me before he went to the Los Angeles Democratic Convention in 1960. We both agreed that L.B.J. would turn down the No. 2 slot.

After Johnson astonished Kennedy, me and the world by accepting the nomination and was duly elected and installed as the Vice President of the United States, I asked him how come he had agreed to take the job, particularly after he had been so vehement with me in his rejection of the idea. "Mr. Sam told me to do it," said Johnson, referring to Speaker of the House Sam Rayburn, a fellow Texan. "He's like a daddy to me. The night before Mr. Sam told me not to do it, Old Jack Garner [the former Vice President] had told him that being V.P. was not worth a boot full of warm piss.

"But next morning after Kennedy's nomination, I was shaving in my hotel bathroom when the door flew open and there was Mr. Sam. 'Lyndon,' he said, 'I want you to accept the vice-presidential nomination.' I was so surprised I cut myself. 'Mr. Sam,' I said, 'why?' Mr. Sam looked at me in the mirror and said, 'Lyndon, I'm a hell of a lot smarter this morning than I was last night.'"

Now, any student of Lyndon Johnson knows that this story could be true or a total fabrication or 10% accurate or 10% inaccurate. Such were the creative ways of L.B.J. They didn't change when he became President. He was a congenital storyteller, and he loved to embellish any fact that came his way. Surprise was his delight, and if he could startle a listener with an exaggerated account of secret events within his White House, he would spring it. That was the origin of the "credibility gap," for the storytelling began to infect other areas of his Administration's policies, like the budget and the war in Vietnam. Trust, the rock on which all leadership is founded, began to be eroded, and Johnson chose to go back home at the end of his only elected term.

When Kennedy was assassinated, Johnson assumed command in the hour of crisis with no hesitation. Master of the ways of Washington, he found the leaders, legislative and executive, in their secret hideaways minutes after Kennedy died; once back in the capital, he summoned them around him and implored them to carry on. "This country needs you now more than when Kennedy was alive," Johnson pleaded

do as a kid back in Johnson City, Texas, and he would mark down the deals made.

He got the leftover bills of the Kennedy era passed, including the first initiative of the new economics—a tax cut during an economic slump. Then he moved on to civil rights and his own Great Society, which roared through a Congress he knew and could persuade and cajole. I walked into the Oval Office one afternoon and he was on the phone and giving some old lady the treatment about her son, a member of Congress. Why, that young man was the best in Washington, he warbled: indeed, he was destined for greatness. When he put the phone down, I asked, "Old friend?" Johnson looked at me incredulously. "Never met the little s.o.b.," he replied.

But Vietnam—half a world away and even farther culturally—was not his beloved Congress, and in its hills and jungles his political skills were useless. A disciple of Franklin Roosevelt's, Johnson wanted to follow the example of his mentor and build dams and roads and houses and bring some dignity and well-being to poor people. And he did that. Then one day he faced a dirty war. He had no experience in that realm; he had no confidants who could advise him on what was phony and what was real in a jungle fight. "I don't understand foreigners," he told reporters on Air Force One flying home after meeting South Vietnam's leaders. "They are different from us." The man next to me leaned close and whispered, "We're in for trouble." He was so right.

The better part of courage in that anguished time might have been to ease off, to find some way to withdraw from an unwinnable war. But Johnson was a proud man. Night after night when he would talk to us about the war, he would bring up the legend of the Alamo, which was just 40 miles from his Hill Country home. "Somebody should have gone to the rescue of those Texans," he would say. "I'm going to Vietnam's rescue. I do not want to be the first President to lose a war." The sad thing was that he did become the first

"I'm going to Vietnam's rescue," he would say, remembering the Texans in the Alamo. "But I do not want to be the first President to lose a war."

with Larry O'Brien, Kennedy's political operative, who would become postmaster general under Johnson. L.B.J. shrouded his own actions in those hours as John Kennedy was mourned and buried so as not to detract from the Kennedys, some of whom were blindly bitter at Johnson, who now had the power that had been theirs. "Get away from that window," Johnson shouted at staff members in his vice-presidential offices across the street from the White House, as Kennedy's furnishings were being trundled out of the Oval Office. "I don't want anybody to say we were eager to move in."

He was a legislative genius, and he knew it. Johnson would summon his old friends like Republican Everett Dirksen down to the White House, and he would pour everyone a drink and then take his list of bills out of his inside coat pocket. For hours he and his cronies would divide up the spoils— a few billion here, a few billion there. L.B.J. would wet the tip of his cedar pencil on his tongue, just as he used to

President to lead us into a losing cause—indeed, the longest and politically one of the most bitter wars that this nation has fought, exceeded in its divisiveness only by the Civil War.

L.B.J. strode the world in seven-league boots, driven by his pride, haughty in his power. He had the biggest fleet of airplanes, helicopters, limousines. Telephones festooned his rooms so he could be in touch with anybody and everybody anywhere. Transportation, technology, even history had to be harnessed to serve his ends. Once, up on the 38th parallel in Korea, where there was still shooting, he talked to the G.I.s on dangerous duty, a splendid-looking group of toughened young men. No doubt, as Johnson talked, he could imagine his heroic self in their midst, a brave comrade in arms. In his speech he told them that his great-grandfather had died at the Alamo. That was pure fiction. But that was the way of L.B.J.: if he said it was so, the facts just might follow the fiction, at least in his mind.   ■

1915

1929

1934

1956

1965

COWBOY Lyndon Johnson was born near Johnson City, named for his grandfather, a pioneer of the region, in the Texas Hill Country on August 27, 1908. His father Sam was a farmer and state legislator; mother Rebekah Baines was the daughter of a lawyer who ran into financial troubles.

TEACHER L.B.J. took a year off from his studies at Southwest Texas State Teachers College to teach poor Mexican children in tiny Cotulla. His anger at social injustice grew, and he told his charges he would someday be President.

HUSBAND Lyndon married Claudia Alta ("Lady Bird") Taylor of Karnack, Texas, the daughter of a well-to-do merchant, in 1934. At the time he was working in Washington as secretary to Austin Congressman Richard Kleberg. L.B.J. made a name for himself with his ambition and intelligence, turning a moribund group of aides, the Little Congress, into a showcase for his leadership.

Texas Dynamo

NEW DEALER An ardent fan of F.D.R.'s, Johnson became chief of the New Deal's National Youth Administration in Texas, then won election to the U.S. House in 1937. Four years later, he lost a special election to fill a U.S. Senate seat, then served in World War II. His Capitol mentor was Speaker Sam Rayburn (left), a fellow Texan.

LEADER After winning a Senate seat in 1948 by 87 votes in a questionable election, "Landslide Lyndon" capped his ascent to power by becoming majority leader in 1953. His methods, as listed by biographer Robert Caro: "... the lapel-grabbing, the embracing, the manipulating of men, the 'wheeling and dealing'"—and his sheer overbearing size, as seen in this picture of L.B.J. towering over longtime ally Abe Fortas.

1967

America: A House Divided

Lyndon Johnson's presidency began in crisis, soared to success and subsided in sorrow

1965

1965

1968

A NATION IN TURMOIL: Lyndon Johnson took the oath of office aboard Air Force One in a moment of grave crisis (below). Drawing upon his keen legislative acumen, he achieved major victories in civil rights, education and health care and easily won election over the G.O.P.'s Barry Goldwater in 1964. But his Vietnam policy left Americans bitterly divided at home—and young American soldiers dying in the jungles of Southeast Asia.

Determined to contain the spread of communism in Asia, L.B.J. began escalating U.S. involvement in Vietnam in 1965. By 1968, 500,000 Americans were in South Vietnam—yet the guerrillas of North Vietnam had the upper hand in the conflict (top left). Meanwhile, Soviet tanks crushed the briefly liberating Prague Spring movement in Czechoslovakia (left) in 1968.

In the streets of America, the Rev. Martin Luther King Jr. led peaceful marchers who were beaten by police in Selma, Alabama, in 1965 (above left). But many blacks rejected nonviolence to demand equal rights—now. Cities erupted in rioting, beginning in the Watts ghetto in Los Angeles in 1965 (bottom left). In March 1968, L.B.J. declared he would not seek re-election. It became one of the most tumultuous years in U.S. history: rioting followed the murder of Dr. King, Bobby Kennedy was killed, and Chicago police beat antiwar protesters during the Democratic Convention.

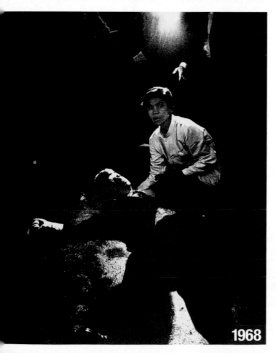

1968

1963

Lady Bird's Crusade for Beauty

First Ladies are still the unsung heroines of the presidency. They must endure the indignities of political campaigning, the dreadful hours of public servants, the criticism aimed at their husbands, and still try to raise families in the midst of this turmoil. Lady Bird Johnson was and is a saint. I never saw a scowl on her face, though she had to put up with the capricious, often outrageous behavior of L.B.J. She left a wonderful mark on the nation as this column points out: in Washington flowers now bloom along the parkways and in public places where in previous years beauty never survived. When I see them I always think of Lady Bird's marvelous smile.

FLOWER POWER The First Lady poses on a Virginia road

THERE IS A LITTLE CONFUSION ABOUT WHO CLIMBED on whose train. Lady Bird Johnson says that the natural-beauty movement in this country had got up steam and was rolling when she got aboard. The gardeners, ornithologists and picnickers say that she laid out the track, stepped up to the throttle and made it all go. Everybody, just about, agrees that it is now a high-balling train. It may be, in fact, that the natural-beauty program is the most successful Great Society venture so far. And it is plain that Mrs. Johnson in the years ahead will be identified with natural beauty in the way Jackie Kennedy is remembered for restoring the White House.

The response to Lady Bird's first plea to preserve and nurture the land was instantaneous and is continuing. At least 200 letters a week come to Lady Bird asking her to settle highway location problems, thanking her because a neighbor was inspired to share her rose bush, and, once, enclosing a batch of delphinium seeds that poured out over the desks of startled secretaries. The mail is called "quality mail" by the White House: it comes on nice paper and is often typed. Some of it is "dollar mail," the true measure of a successful campaign. There are letters like the one from G.E. offering advice about burying power lines to give neighborhoods a neat look.

The phones ring too. One Washingtonian figured that Lady Bird could handle any problem, and when he saw a plant wilting in one of the parks he called and urged some sprinkling. Such confidence is not misplaced. When one Ohioan wrote complaining of some unsightly airplane hulks at Wright-Patterson Air Force Base, Mrs. Johnson brought the letter to the Secretary of Defense, who was dining at the White House that evening. In 24 hours the planes had been ordered behind a grove of trees. Builders in the Washington area suddenly discovered this spring that they could not get a decent-sized azalea bush within 70 miles of the capital: the beautification program had cleaned out the markets.

Lady Bird has long been known for her shrewd financial instincts. And she hasn't forgotten them in her pursuit of beauty. She is quick to remind people what Shell Oil discovered—that attractively landscaped filling stations in many instances outsold those decorated with balloons and pennants. Ladies apparently determine a large number of the motor stops and figure that stations with shade trees probably have more appealing rest rooms too. Factory owners have reported that landscaping has helped cut down on personnel turnover.

All 5 ft. 3 in. of Lady Bird are in this fight. With an eye to her beautification tasks, she selects dresses with the A-line design so that she can get her foot up on a shovel. The others are too tight for these earthy tasks, so she always packs a few of her "tree-planting dresses." Because planting season seems to come with rain, the Lady Bird entourage goes forth equipped with umbrellas and slickers. Local residents can distinguish a beauty safari when it sets out from the White House because the end of the line is often brought up by a well-muscled Secret Service man carrying a potted White House seedling to be planted somewhere.

Lady Bird has one nagging worry. She wants words that better express the movement. Natural beauty, beautification, conservation—those terms are part of it but not all of what the movement is after. New York's Mary Lasker got close when she said of Mrs. Johnson, "She's lifted the spirits of everyone." And the President himself had a good thought one day as he surveyed the acres of wildflowers his wife had sown all over his ranch and remarked with gruff delight, "She's going to beuatify us right out of existence." What a way to go. ∎

Pondering the State of the Man

When Lyndon Johnson went home to his Texas ranch in 1969 he was under the cloud of the failed war in Vietnam. Now there is a new appreciation for what he accomplished in the Great Society legislation, which he shepherded through Congress. He did more for civil rights than any President since Lincoln. He sponsored more than a hundred education programs, won passage of Medicare and Medicaid. As the memory of the divisive Vietnam War fades, those achievements take on new luster.

DISAGREE WITH HIM, DENOUNCE HIM, HONOR HIM, rib him, praise him, ridicule him, give up on him, be embarrassed and insulted by him, degraded by him, and honored by him, overwhelmed and frightened by him, and struggle with him that way for 10 years from Senate to White House. Then stand down there on the floor of the House of Representatives on the night of the 181st State of the Union address and see President Lyndon B. Johnson, lined and grayed and worried and yet confident and, above all, enduring. Then you have to—for a moment as the applause from the Congress, the Supreme Court, the ambassadors and Joint Chiefs and anybody that matters in this government begins to swell around you— then you and a lot of others have to call off that necessary rivalry between press and public servant and pay a silent tribute to a worthy adversary who stands there in the fire pit of government by the people for the people.

You recall the night that he stalked you around a table in his Capitol office and bellowed his outrage at something you wrote, "You're a whore for the Republican Party." A chuckle escapes your lips now.

The time he erupted over the story about his driving 90 m.p.h. down at the ranch while sipping Pearl beer from a paper cup: "They warp everything I do, they lie about me and about what I do, they don't know the meaning of truth." And the final jab: "That wasn't Pearl beer. I never had it on the ranch." There is something marvelously warm about the memory just now.

"There are half a dozen newsmen who don't like me. They call me a buffoon and a politician. But I like all of them." How could he say it, you wonder, and then you think maybe he understands this thing called the freedom of the press better than you realized.

You muffle a laugh when you remember the time he showed his gall-bladder scar in front of a battery of cameras and, when the picture went out all over the world, looked innocent and incredulous and said of the camera-

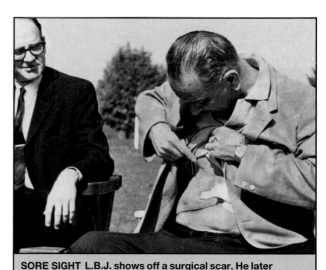

SORE SIGHT L.B.J. shows off a surgical scar. He later feigned amazement that newspapers ran the picture

men, "Now, why did they do that to me?" And the time he denied that he ever told painter Peter Hurd that his portrait of L.B.J. was "the ugliest thing I ever saw." What did you say, Mr. President? "I said, 'It's hideous'" You look up at him, waiting in front of everybody, ready to speak.

There are remembered bursts of rough lightning from that tumultuous decade. "We can't let Goldwater and Red China both get the bomb at the same time. Then it would really hit the fan." That said a lot in the campaign of 1964. "When a President is elected he is a giraffe, after six months a worm." Right again. The time he was belabored for picking people from the ranks of government to fill the top openings, instead of getting in fresh blood. "I like to do it that way. It inspires the others. It's like that Texas politician who said that his election 'has inspired every ignoramus in East Texas.'" A little jarring, yes. But you are glad he said it.

You cast an eye out over the floor at others who have had some intense relationships with the President. In the second row, beside Georgia's Richard Russell, is Senator William Fulbright. "He's the stud duck of the opposition," Johnson once snorted. Stud duck is furrowed, chewing gum, cracking knuckles. He must be paying at least a little tribute too.

What about the "babies," L.B.J.'s term for the Kennedy Senators? Teddy is not here, but Bobby is in the fourth row, wary but attentive. Even the baby gave a salute, slapping his hand on his knee as applause. The President begins to speak and you look again and there he is, a hulk of raw strength and hope bound for somewhere. "I report to you that our country is challenged, at home and abroad ..." ■

COMMANDER IN CHIEF

Presidents often say that the most serious burden of their office is their role as Commander in Chief of the nation's armed forces. But many have earned their stripes: 20th century Presidents have included one five-star general, Dwight D. Eisenhower, and two authentic war heroes—John Kennedy and George Bush.

GESTURE OF SUPPORT

George Bush tosses souvenirs to U.S.
troops serving in Saudi Arabia in Operation
Desert Shield, Thanksgiving, 1990.

THE BURDEN

Lyndon Johnson anguished over his escalation of the Vietnam War—and he was not insulated from its effects. In the picture at left, taken July 31, 1968, the President has just listened to a tape recording made by his son-in-law, Captain Charles Robb Jr., then serving in Vietnam. On the recording, Robb described his distress at watching young Americans die in battle.

THE SURPRISE

On April 11, 1951, Harry Truman relieved World War II legend General Douglas MacArthur of his command in Korea—though the two had been all smiles at an October 1950 meeting on Wake Island, above. Truman would write in his memoirs: "I could no longer tolerate his insubordination." At right, General Dwight D. Eisenhower hears the news.

BOX LUNCH

With U.S. troops locked in a stalemated "police action" in Korea in 1952, G.O.P. candidate Dwight D. Eisenhower, the mastermind of D-day, caught voters' imagination with his vow that, if elected, he would go to Korea to inspect the U.S. troops and their situation. A month after the election, he made good on his promise—even before taking the oath of office. Here Ike shares rations—pork chops and sauerkraut— with members of his old outfit, the 1st Battalion, 15th Regiment, 3rd Infantry Division.

MISSION TO MOROCCO

Franklin Roosevelt reviews American troops in
Casablanca in January 1943 after arriving for a war
conference with Winston Churchill. Roosevelt mastered
military affairs early in his career; he was Assistant
Secretary of the Navy from 1913 to 1920. But he never
served in uniform: though he sought to resign from his
position and enlist during World War I, President
Woodrow Wilson refused his appeal. However,
Roosevelt was pleased when he was sent on a mission to
review American operations in Europe in 1918.

ATTENTION!

Many Presidents learned to salute from the ground (or sea) up. **Left,** Captain Harry Truman in France, 1918, as a member of Battery D, 129th Field Artillery. **Right,** Lieut. (j.g.) John Kennedy aboard P.T. 109 in 1943; he proved his courage after the craft sank off the Solomon Islands. **Below,** Lieut. (j.g.) George Bush is hauled aboard the submarine U.S.S. *Finback* after his TBM Avenger, *Barbara,* was shot down in 1944.

PERILOUS DAYS

Jimmy Carter and
Dwight Eisenhower
are the only two 20th
century Presidents
to graduate from
military academies.
Left, after Annapolis,
Lieut. (j.g.) Carter,
front row, served
aboard the U.S.S.
Wyoming in 1947.
Right, Lieut. Richard
Nixon served on
Bouganville in the
South Pacific, 1943-44.
Above, Lieut. Gerald
Ford is the sailor on
the left jumping for a
basketball on the air-
craft carrier U.S.S.
Monterey in 1944.

MORALE BOOSTER

Richard Nixon took office in January 1969, as the war in Vietnam bitterly divided Americans. In his memoirs, Nixon wrote, "I knew that I was assuming the role of Commander in Chief at what was perhaps the most troubled time in the history of our armed forces. Never before had our fighting men been subjected to such criticism—and never to such obloquy—during wartime." Left, Nixon visits soldiers on a surprise trip to South Vietnam later that year.

HAIL FROM THE CHIEF

Ronald Reagan, a great advocate of military might, presided over a massive buildup of America's armed forces during the endgame of the cold war. Above, the President salutes sailors aboard the aircraft carrier U.S.S. *Constellation* in August 1981. Reagan did not see combat in World War II: he served in the army's motion-picture unit, helping to make training films. He later appeared in several Hollywood war movies.

San Clemente, California, 1971

Richard M. Nixon

A visionary strategist who relished his place on the world stage, he became the architect of his own downfall

RICHARD NIXON GAVE THIS NATION A POLITical roller-coaster ride for most of a half-century. It astonishes me now as I look back to note that I wrote more about Nixon—and over a longer period—than about any other President. I'm still not done.

Only a few months ago, rooting through the ghostly memos of the long-defunct Nixon Administration, I uncovered a half-inch stack of directives aimed at me: Keep him off Air Force One; no interviews to Sidey; make up a letter from a fictional reader urging him to be less critical. There may be no escape from this singular character, in this world or the next.

My first encounter with Nixon was indelible. He was Vice President, and I found my way to one of his many Capitol Hill offices, this one in the Senate Office Building. He was ensconced at his desk behind a huge maroon drape, something like the Wizard of Oz. I've long forgotten the conversation of that day; certainly it involved nothing alarming. But I do recall the flawless white shirt he wore, and the knife-edged creases of his gray suit. It would always be so. We reporters sometimes joked that Nixon must

bathe in a stiff white shirt. But after 1960 such personal speculations were of minor moment, since his defeat in the presidential election seemed to confine him to history's dustbin. Were we ever wrong.

President Nixon came in three distinct acts: the global strategic genius who sensed it was time to welcome China back into the family of nations; the political conniver who brought us the Watergate scandal and vainly tried to cover it up; and, at the end, the scarred and mellowed warrior tramping around the world in his crepe-soled shoes, looking and listening for the creaks and groans of developing societies, reporting it all back to whichever President would listen.

China was the pinnacle. Some 450 million people, a fourth of the world's population, had in 1949 turned inward to build the perfect communist society. No U.S. politician had been more vehement in his denunciations of those who had "lost" China than Richard Nixon; no national leader in the subsequent years was more direct in his condemnation of the "Red Chinese" than Nixon. Yet on a bright February day in 1972, a smiling Nixon descended the ramp of Air Force One in Beijing and gripped the hand of Zhou Enlai, China's Premier. It was mind-boggling.

We stood in this strange land so far away from Washington in the heart of the "enemy's" bastion. But there were no military forces lined up, no SWAT teams lurking in the bushes. The world had turned. It was eerily quiet for a city airport. A band played, there was the cadence of an honor guard; no airplanes took off or landed during this brief ceremony. We could hear birds chirping in the distant trees, and then there was the muted hum of bicycles, thousands of bicycles on the dusty streets.

We should have seen this grand diplomatic maneuver coming. Nixon had hinted at it a dozen times in the preceding months. Once, at an interview with a group of TIME reporters and editors, he had exclaimed wistfully, "If there is anything I want to do before I die, it is to go to China. If I

around Zhou and then clinked a glass of champagne with him. It was the high water mark of Nixon's prestige and power. Watergate lay just a few months down the road.

The descent into squalor and then the resignation of Nixon remain a mystery of the human soul. For all the books that have been written on Watergate, none can authoritatively unlock the inner dilemma. Did Nixon order the break-in and bugging of the phones at the Democratic National Committee? Did he know about it and give tacit consent? Was he victimized by dunderheaded staffers? I concluded that he probably did know about the break-in ahead of time, but he was constitutionally incapable of admitting it. Such a confession might have wrecked him as a man after he wove his elaborate skein of denials, which I suspect he actually began to believe after a time.

I watched the melancholy tableau of August 1974, going to the White House as often as I could to see the few staff members who maintained contact with the press. Once I met Al Haig, who had stepped in as emergency chief of Nixon's White House staff. We talked in the shadowy Map Room, the ground-floor chamber that Franklin Roosevelt and Winston Churchill had used to plan World War II. Richard Nixon's presidency was over, Haig said, that mystical bond with the people broken, trust lost for all time. The task was to see that Nixon understood this and to find as graceful an exit as possible under the wretched circumstances.

When I walked back out on the White House lawn, I turned to look at the old mansion I had seen in so many

We stood in this strange land so far away, in the heart of the "enemy's" bastion ... The world had turned. It was eerily quiet for a city airport

don't, I want my children to." We did not tumble even then to the fact that Nixon was searching for a back channel through which he could secretly schedule this summit.

I had listened to Lyndon Johnson yearn for some way to get the Chinese to a negotiating table so he could "see them and hear them." He asked rhetorically in one interview, "If we don't talk, how are we going to settle our differences?" Then he added, rather sadly, "But my diplomats tell me I can't do it." Nixon told his diplomats what he wanted, not the other way around.

After the awesome silence of the afternoon in Beijing, we went to the Great Hall and the intriguing drama continued. Many of the old military leaders who had taken the Long March with Chairman Mao Zedong, who was now ailing, mingled with the Americans. A People's Liberation Army band tootled reasonable renditions of *America the Beautiful* and *Turkey in the Straw.* A jubilant Nixon threw his arms

crises. Strange, no President I had known had so coveted the White House as Nixon. No President ever had been forced to give it up before his time. I wondered if he would live long once separated from the office he loved.

Nixon entered a twilight period, withdrawing for six years to his seaside home in San Clemente, California. Then he eased back into the world, moved east and became a high-profile nomad. There was one last lunch a few years before his death. We sat in his meticulous town house in Park Ridge, New Jersey, and he talked about the friends he had made in his wanderings through Soviet flower markets and butcher shops: splendid, strong people, he said, who before long would junk communism. "The Soviet Union is an empty shell," he added. "Now it is just a question of when it will fall apart." I noticed that Richard Nixon had on a stiff white shirt, and his gray suit was pressed to perfection. And, of course, he was right about the Soviet Union. ∎

1913

1934

California Quaker

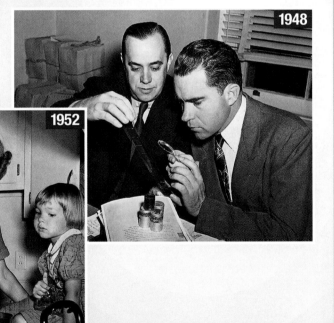

1948

1952

1959

EARLY DAYS Richard Nixon was born on January 9, 1913, in Yorba Linda, California, the second of five sons, two of whom died in youth. Father Frank owned a service station and market in Whittier where Richard worked from an early age; mother Hannah Milhous helped out too. "It was not an easy life," Nixon wrote, "but it was a good one, centered around a loving family and a small, tight-knit Quaker community."

STUDENT A top scholar in high school, Nixon yearned to attend an Eastern college, but family finances did not permit it. He attended Whittier College, where he was a debater and football player (center). He won a scholarship to the new Duke University School of Law and then returned to Whittier to practice. In December 1941 he got a job in the Office of Price Administration in Washington. He joined the Navy in 1942 and served in the South Pacific.

CONGRESS Nixon was elected to Congress in 1946 from California's 12th District. In the era of the "red scare," the rabid anticommunist quickly made a name for himself on the House Un-American Activities Committee and in the case of accused spy Alger Hiss.

FAMILY Nixon married Patricia Ryan in 1940; they had met in an amateur theater group. A University of Southern California graduate, she had worked in New York City and as a movie extra. Daughter Tricia was born in 1946, Julie in 1948.

VEEP Elected to the Senate in 1950, Nixon caught the eye of Dwight Eisenhower and joined the G.O.P. ticket in 1952. Under attack, he defended his dog Checkers and other donations from backers in a TV speech. As Vice President, he was not close to Ike but scored points in the "kitchen debate" with Nikita Khrushchev at a U.S. trade exhibit in Moscow.

1970

Lunar Joys, Earthly Woes

In Richard Nixon's America, the only tranquillity to be found was on the moon

1974

1969

1969

LAW AND ORDER: Borne into office on the appeal of his vow to restore "law and order" to an America riven by riots and protest, Richard Nixon claimed he would be a healer, and he was soon able to bask in the triumph of America's great victory in the space race: Apollo 11's landing on the moon's Sea of Tranquillity on July 20, 1969. The next month, more than 400,000 hippies shared peace and love at the Woodstock music festival in upstate New York. But the good vibes in space (and among spaced-out kids) soon gave way to renewed antiwar fervor.

Nixon had said during his election that he would scale down U.S. involvement in Vietnam, but "Vietnamization" of the war was slow; it was not completed until 1973. In the meantime, Nixon's decision in April 1970 to send U.S. troops into Cambodia (below) in what he called a "limited incursion" heightened antiwar protest. During protests at Kent State University in Ohio, four students were killed by Ohio National Guardsmen (top left).

After his dramatic visit to China in 1972, Nixon trounced George McGovern to win re-election. The next year, the Supreme Court's decision to legalize abortion in the *Roe* v. *Wade* case opened a deep divide in American culture that remains a source of contention almost three decades later (bottom left). Ironically, Nixon's "law and order" presidency expired in the criminal, self-inflicted debacle of Watergate.

1970

Trying to Ensure an Epitaph

SHIPWRECKED In the end, Nixon turned to Kissinger, the man who had helped shape his triumphs, as his closest confidant

At some point during the last convulsions of Richard Nixon's presidency, I ran into White House chief of staff Alexander Haig. "Nixon will be dead within a year," he said. I agreed. How could a person who prided himself so much on his understanding of the exercise of power survive the humiliation of being forced from office? We were both wrong. Nixon rebounded from his ordeal and continued to be a best-selling author and expert on foreign policy and leadership in the modern world.

SOME DAY HISTORY MAY RANK THEM AS SPECIAL heroes, emerging out of a shadowy world of anguish that now we can only begin to comprehend. Alexander Haig, the President's chief of staff, who, with deep care and sensitivity, midwifed the political death of Richard Nixon. James St. Clair, reviled by many when he went before the Supreme Court and the Congress, who finally recognized there was no defense of the President and told him so. Henry Kissinger, who came into Nixon's orbit of power as the lone outsider, but who in the end was comforter, friend and the man to whom Nixon entrusted his one hope—that he be remembered as a man of peace.

Perhaps no story like this has ever been written. Kings

have gone. Dictators have been forced out. But there has never been a man of such power, a man of such renown, a man elected by 47 million people, who gave it all away.

It was Wednesday, July 31, when Haig learned of the evidence that would end Nixon's career [the so-called smoking-gun tapes revealing Nixon's early complicity in the cover-up of the burglary, which he had long denied— Ed.]. Haig hurried through the humid streets of Washington to Kissinger's State Department office. He told Kissinger what had been found. It was a curious time for these two old friends who had been through so much together. It was a time of relief, surely. They had talked many times before, and vaguely in the distance, they had seen the end approaching, even without the new tapes. Now it was real, and rushing in on them.

They had no choice. Their loyalty, and the loyalty of the others who stood around Nixon, had to be lifted beyond that one personality. It had to be fixed on the office of the President, on the United States of America. Nixon somehow had to be shepherded through the ordeal so that he understood and would not ravage himself even more in futile resistance.

Kissinger kept in touch with James Schlesinger, Secretary of Defense, and William Simon, Secretary of the

Treasury, the two other most powerful and visible Cabinet members. Their understanding was that the Cabinet must be calmed, must be kept in touch with reality. A careless speech or comment on fighting it out might falsely mislead Nixon about the inevitability of resignation, might freeze him into a position that would grow even more tragic. In Haig's frantic orchestration were the Republican Congressmen and the Republican Senators, men whose voices would mean something in bringing the light to Nixon.

Haig, St. Clair and their few allies walked on eggs through the last weekend at Camp David, responding instead of telling, implying more than explaining. With his family gathered around him, all of whom wanted to fight it out, Nixon still did not believe that beyond the White House cocoon the world had turned so hard against him.

On his yacht, cruising the Potomac Monday night, he was the tough field marshal, devising some grand strategy that would roll it all back in one brilliant stroke so that he could stand vindicated in some distant place and time. He put it bluntly the next day at the Cabinet meeting. He would not resign. There were no protests. But for the first time there were no spontaneous expressions of joy about fighting the good battle. The absence of cheers for his defiance may have helped make things come more clearly into focus for Richard Nixon. He asked Kissinger to see him after the Cabinet meeting. History will tell the story someday. We can only assume it was then that the man who had carried the faltering Nixon credibility so far by his own genius and honor said, face to face, that he felt that for everybody's good, Nixon should resign.

Then the legacy of peace suddenly became uppermost in Nixon's mind, and in the minds of all these men. Haig, Kissinger and the others wanted to save that much for Nixon. If there was to be an epitaph, Nixon wanted it thus. Kissinger emerged to tell the world that American foreign policy stood unchanged. It would go on, just as America was going on.

On Tuesday evening Nixon was coming to grips with hard reality. He called Kissinger five times on the phone. He talked about his position: what would happen in the world, the country, if he stayed, if he went. He was a man reaching for any support, yet knowing there was none, or at least beginning to perceive it. He was a man trying to fashion something graceful from the terrible debris that, as in a Greek tragedy, he had created.

Someplace there must be a log of the number of times Nixon met with Haig and Kissinger, but they could not keep track. By Wednesday night Nixon's mind was fixed. He would go. He told his family.

Kissinger was asked to the mansion late Wednesday after the President had had his dinner. Nixon wanted to talk one last time as President, one last time as they used to talk when they so joyfully contemplated the world and saw their great plans succeeding.

Nixon told Kissinger that he would resign the next day. Nixon talked on; he talked about many things. He talked about his family and about his Quakerism, and about peace and how deeply he believed in it. He talked about prayer and some will beyond his. He wanted to know if he would be remembered for bringing world peace in his years as President. Henry Kissinger told him that he would be.

There are few historic moments that could exceed this in intensity and pain and sorrow. The most powerful man in the world was giving up his power, which he had devoted his life to achieving. The man in whom he had placed the most trust in the use of that power was listening, and was somehow trying to make it right or at best bearable.

What thoughts must go through those minds? Again, we can only begin to imagine. But Kissinger must have sensed the irony of it all. Richard Nixon, the immensely complex figure in front of him, had done all the things that eventually brought him down out of his general aspirations for good. If Nixon had only hated totally, it might have been easier. But he was not that simple. He craved the adoration of the press and the Eastern liberals even as he assaulted them. He coveted the public trust even as he withdrew from people. He espoused the ideals of a democratic society even as he violated them.

GOOD SHEPHERDS Alexander Haig and James St. Clair worked together to help ease Nixon out of office with dignity

It was after midnight when they parted. Kissinger went back to his office in the West Wing of the White House. The phone rang. Nixon wanted to talk some more, a kind of last, thin reach for a life that was ebbing. Then sometime between midnight and 1 a.m. as far as anyone knows, Richard Nixon cut himself off from the outside world and returned to his family to wait for the daylight. ∎

Washington, 1974

Gerald R. Ford

After Watergate, he restored our trust in the presidency and healed America's wounds—but the price was his office

W E COULD FEEL IT COMING ALL WEEK. Richard Nixon's presidency was in its death throes. On August 8, 1974, a Thursday, the word was out that Nixon would give a nationwide television address that night, and presumably he would announce his intention to resign from the office the next day. Or would he? There were still doubts, right up until the end.

I walked over to Lafayette Park on that warm and sultry evening, and it was almost filled with people watching the White House, which glowed in its floodlights. Cars hurried in and out, and occasionally a staff aide loped along the walks. A huge press contingent had assembled on the front lawn and some journalists, like CBS's Dan Rather, spilled over into the park. Nothing like this had happened in the 200-year history of the United States of America.

Many of the people just stood mute, not quite knowing how they should feel about the disgrace of a President. Some sobbed and clutched each other. Many cheered, believing the American system was purging itself of a villain. Rather and other correspondents would leap up on a chair every now and then, face a camera and inform the nation in breathless tones that we had reached the climax of the Watergate scandal.

I stood in the park with Peter Lisagor, correspondent for the Chicago *Daily News;* we were both friendly with Vice President Gerald Ford. We studied the Old Executive Office Building, where Ford had his office, the lights blazing through the thick air. Nobody could really see anything. In fact, Ford had already left the office to go to his home in Alexandria, Virginia, where he would watch with his family as Nixon handed him the presidency.

From time immemorial, when crisis has struck, citizens of Washington have come to the White House, as if drawn by some mystical force. More often than not they have just stood in silence in front of the gates, feeling that by their presence they were bolstering their country. Once, on Pearl Harbor day, they began to sing *God Bless America.* There were no such songs on this August night.

"What do you suppose old Jerry is thinking now?" Pete asked. "A few months ago, he was nothing but a down-at-the-heels Congressman from Michigan. Now look: he is about to become President of the most

said after he had taken the oath of office: "My fellow Americans, our long national nightmare is over."

He made sure of that a month later when he pardoned Nixon, creating a fire storm of criticism. Ford never wavered in his conviction that it had been the right move. "Can you imagine what it would have been like to have a sick and disgraced President in the dock for months on end?" Ford asked me later. "We had to get on with the country's business."

The pardon may have cost Ford re-election to the presidency in 1976, but he never whined. Indeed, history moved to his side. In 1999 Ford was awarded the Congressional Gold Medal, and President Bill Clinton in his tribute explained he had been critical of the Nixon pardon at the time, but his view had changed. "You were right," said Clinton, turning toward Ford, "and I thank you for that." The hundreds of people in the Capitol erupted in applause.

If Jerry Ford was never intimidated by power and its responsibilities, he also was never blinded by pride or arrogance. He had never imagined he would be Vice President and then President, executive positions. He was a creature of the House of Representatives, and he had worked his way up to minority leader. Until Nixon's White House began to unravel, the only other job Ford dreamed about was winning the Speaker's seat in a Republican-majority House. The thought of assuming executive responsibilities outside of running his legislative offices had eluded him.

So he listened—and he turned to the men and women around him he knew to be experts on the myriad subjects that rush across a President's desk every 24 hours. Ford never hesitated to admit his lack of expertise. He had seen too many leaders confronted with complex issues pretend an under-

The world will long remember what Ford said after he had taken the oath of office: "My fellow Americans, our long national nightmare is over"

powerful nation in the world. How do you figure any of this? You don't. You just ride along and somehow it works out."

Ford would tell me later that he was never frightened that night—or any other—at the prospect of being President. He did not feel overwhelmed by the job that was passed to him. Concerned, of course. Apprehensive a bit. Wondering. All of those things. But many years before, he had become toughened to political crisis. He had been at the heart of history for 26 years and had seen most of the world's top leaders up close. They were not gods. He had dealt with every President since Harry Truman, who had asked Ford down to look over the crumbling interior of the White House and he had helped Truman get $5 million to rebuild the insides. Presidents, Ford had concluded long ago, were people, perhaps a little special but not with superhuman powers.

His walk to the departing helicopter the next day with the Nixons was one of the most difficult single moments in his life. He was with an old friend, a disgraced old friend, a humiliated former President. "What do you say," he once remarked to me. "I didn't know what to say. I can't remember what I said." But the world remembered what President Ford

standing they did not possess, always a hazardous posture.

Only a few months after taking office, Ford and Secretary of State Henry Kissinger flew to Vladivostok on the Pacific coast of the U.S.S.R. to talk to Soviet boss Leonid Brezhnev about limiting the number of nuclear weapons, an arcane and perplexing process even to the experts. The summit was peopled by the usual crews of bureaucrats and press from both sides, the Soviet press corps heavy with KGB case agents masquerading as reporters.

I was lounging outside the meeting room with other Americans when the first session broke up and the staff members came out to brief the press. I noted on the Soviet side a lot of winking, and some snickers. One of the "reporters" sidled up to me and whispered, "What kind of President is Ford? He doesn't know anything about disarmament. Whenever he is asked a question about missiles or nuclear warheads, he turns to Henry Kissinger and asks him to answer."

As I recall, several of us broke into broad smiles and replied, "That's the best news we've heard yet about Jerry Ford. He's not going to fake it." I suspect that our friends in the Soviet "press" are still scratching their heads. ∎

1918

1933

STEPSON Gerald Ford was born Leslie Lynch King Jr. on July 14, 1913, in Omaha, Nebraska. After his parents divorced in 1915, his mother moved to Grand Rapids, Michigan, remarried and gave her son the name of his step-father Gerald Ford, a paint salesman. Three half brothers were born later. The Fords prospered, but suffered in the market crash of 1929. Gerald did not know he was adopted until his real father paid him a surprise visit when he was 17.

Man from Michigan

1948

1964

1974

ATHLETE Better at sports than studies, Jerry was a star center in high school football, earning a scholarship to the University of Michigan, where he was again a star—and his grades improved. Hired to help coach the Yale University football and boxing teams, he wangled entry to the Law School and graduated in the top third of his class in 1941.

WAR AND PEACE Ford joined the Navy in 1942 and served in the South Pacific, seeing a good deal of action. He went back to Michigan to practice law and married Elizabeth Bloomer Warren, a divorcé, in 1948. Betty was a former student of dancer Martha Graham's; she and Jerry had four children.

G.O.P. LEADER Ford was elected to Congress in 1948, after beating a four-term incumbent in Michigan's 5th District in the G.O.P. primary. Popular and respected, he served until 1973. L.B.J. asked him to serve on the Warren Commission in 1963, left, and Ford became House minority leader in '65.

FILLING IN Known for his honesty, the minority leader was Richard Nixon's pick to replace Spiro Agnew, who resigned as Vice President in 1973. At left, Ford and Nixon confer the day before Nixon resigned and Ford stepped in.

1975

Pardon, Panic and Pomp

Gerald Ford ended Nixon's saga and oversaw Saigon's fall and America's big bash

NO MORE PARDONS

PARDON NIX

Herald Tribune

1974

1975

MAYAGUEZ

1976

1975

1976

HAPPY BIRTHDAY! Gerald Ford's presidency began in joy: after the seemingly endless Watergate affair, Americans hailed the new President as a healer and straight shooter. The honeymoon proved short lived. Less than five weeks after Nixon resigned, Ford granted him a complete pardon—and the streets again were filled with protesters (bottom left).

Ford's abbreviated term saw moments of both grandeur and despair. In a low point in American history, Saigon, the capital of South Vietnam, fell to communist troops in April 1975, ending the long American misadventure there in terrible scenes of civilians fighting to board U.S. aircraft to evacuate the country (top left). The next month, Ford acted quickly to strike back at Cambodian terrorists who had seized the U.S. merchant ship *Mayaguez*.

At home, the nation's ongoing battles over race infected Boston, where the busing of schoolchildren to achieve integration sparked rioting in a number of predominantly white areas of the city in 1975 (left).

In 1976 Americans at last found something to cheer about. NASA's Viking 1 probe successfully landed on Mars in July—the same month the U.S. celebrated its 200th birthday with a sail-in of tall ships to New York Harbor (above) and a host of patriotic festivities across the nation.

He Has Done His Homework

OFFENSIVE ACTION Gerald Ford stages an impromptu driveway press conference to defend his energy policy

Gerald Ford was the right man in the right place at the right time. The national affection for him has increased with the passing years. His common sense and his good heart saved this nation from unnecessary anguish as so many sought vengeance after Watergate. He may have sacrificed his re-election because he pardoned Richard Nixon and moved the country beyond that turmoil.

THE COUNTRY HAD A PRESIDENT LAST WEEK, AND IT was such a novel experience that a lot of people were not sure what to make of it. Gerald Ford was acting like a real leader. He was the only man in town with a complete economic and energy plan, and whether it will ultimately be judged good or bad, he was moving ahead with relish and considerable skill.

After attending about 100 solid hours of meetings on these matters over the past two months and consuming literally millions of written words on the intricate issues, the President clearly knew his subject better than his critics. That is considered unsportsmanlike conduct in these gaseous climes.

Carl Albert, the Speaker of the House, went to breakfast with reporters and was so mixed up about Ford's plan that he admitted he had not studied it. "We're talking about thousands of little pieces of paper," Albert said, believing that taxpayers would have to get receipts for gasoline and turn them in for tax rebates. No, no, said

reporters, that wasn't the plan. "Well, how is he going to do that ... I don't know," said Albert.

Ten Governors (eight of them Democrats) from the Northeastern states came to town breathing fire, claiming that the Ford energy tax would penalize their states. They circled around Ford in the Cabinet Room for what one claimed was "a very hard talking session." Massachusetts' Michael Dukakis was the toughest, boring in with a list of arguments against Ford's proposals. Finally, in a stern voice, he asked Ford, "Have you considered the unfairness of what you're about to do?" "I'm sorry," came back Ford, "I disagree with you ... we've looked at every possible option. They were piled high ... we were on the threshold of disaster ... we have got to have action."

Ford looked Dukakis in the eye and hammered the table as he spoke. He listened to each of the Governors as they made their complaints. The meeting ran 30 minutes beyond schedule, but Ford heard them all out. When it was over he went to his small study, and one of his aides murmured, "That was really rough." Ford showed no bitterness. "I've got to hear that," he said. "They've got their problems, and I want to know about them."

But then Ford strode into the Oval Office to sign the very proclamation, to increase the oil-import fees, that the Governors had opposed. He made his statement somberly, scribbled his left-handed signature, then, looking up at the silent gallery of aides, newsmen and photographers, chuckled, "I don't see anybody clamoring for extra pens."

At that time the Governors were using the White House lawn to denounce the Ford plan before the TV cameras. It was hard talk, but it was civilized, the kind of ritual on which good government thrives. Ford's staff members reported back to him what was happening out front. Rather than hide in his sanctum, the President decided to go out on the lawn and rebut the critics. Instantly, he had a driveway press conference going. "We've diddled and dawdled long enough," he said. "We have to have an energy program ... I think the American people want action ... affirmative action, not negative action."

By the end of the day he was sitting in the family quarters of the White House, having just finished an hour of live-television questioning by NBC's John Chancellor and Tom Brokaw. The TV lights were out, the cameras dead, and the men were sipping Scotches. Ford was puffing his pipe and musing about the people who were going after him. Ford was handicapping each of those who would oppose him, determined to press his case in a democratic manner. It is such a sane and decent approach that it has already confounded a sizable segment of the population. ■

"This Is the Toughest"

This interview with Gerald Ford took place as he was battling Ronald Reagan to win the G.O.P. presidential nomination and anticipating a fall campaign against the rising Jimmy Carter. Ford won the nomination but lost the general election. He would say later that if the campaign had gone another two weeks, he would have defeated Carter. Perhaps, but Ford probably carried too much of the burden of the Watergate scandal to push himself over the top, even if he had had two more weeks.

THERE WAS A TOUCH OF UNCLE JERRY ABOUT THE President when he talked of Ronald Reagan and Jimmy Carter last week. Reagan was a professional performer. "That's been his life," mused Ford in the Oval Office. "He's been very skillful in picking several very emotional issues," he continued. "And the combination of his performance and the use of certain issues has generated a lot of public support ... but I certainly hold no grudge against my Republican opponent, and I don't believe he does as far as I am concerned."

And Jimmy Carter? "It just doesn't seem to me that he's ready for this big league," said Ford. Right then in the Oval Office, it was so quiet the ticking of the grandfather clock sounded like a hammer. "I don't think he is dangerous," mused Ford. "I don't think he is focused on the complexities of the problems we have, or ready to face up to the hard decisions that have to be made." Didn't he like the Carter smile? "It doesn't bother me."

Defeat? "I have not even considered the possibility," Ford said. He had never talked it over with Betty or with the kids. No, he said, never. But when pressed, he allowed as how he could be defeated and still hold his head up. "I have absolute confidence in the decisions I have made. If you feel you've done the right thing, defeat doesn't gnaw at you; it doesn't keep you from sleeping at night." He could go back to Grand Rapids, he nodded, if necessary.

Some 28 years and 14 campaigns ago, he thought he might get beaten because he was running against a nine-year incumbent Congressman. He beat him. "From that time on, I never had any race where I got less than 60% of the vote," he said. "This is the toughest." But within a month of becoming President he decided he would stay on the job, "that I would stay and fight it out and get elected in November of 1976." He could trace his current political dilemma all the way back to the first days when he came into the White House, Ford explained. He wanted from the start to get away from "the old politics, maybe start a new course where I could honestly say that I wasn't promising more than I was producing ... I believe that I have followed that pretty well—made hard choices that weren't necessarily political choices."

But that was not Reagan's style, was it? "What has he done?" Ford challenged. "He promised a $90 billion reduction in the federal budget. There is not a man in government or the news media that believes he can produce on that. There isn't one. That's a variation of the old politics, but it is the same thing."

There was no real anger against anybody. Not the primary system, not the press, not the world. Ford's faith in his party is basically sound, perhaps dented. "There is a hard core in the party that is very dedicated but very much in the right wing. They get out and do the job, have deep feeling. But they don't represent the broad spectrum of the middle of the road, where I think most Americans are ... The tragedy is that part of the spectrum of the party doesn't have the same zeal to go to party caucuses, go to the conventions, even to get out the vote ... The people in the middle are sort of apathetic. How to regenerate them—we haven't found an answer."

Ford sipped his iced tea. The afternoon light began to fade across the south lawn. He had had his ups and downs over the last week. He was a bit more tired than usual, just

ON THE HUSTINGS Ford strikes an exuberant pose at a primary rally in Holland, Michigan; wife Betty is on the right

a shade more subdued. But he was still a believer. "I'm an optimist," he said. "It's a great thrill being President ... Betty and I are well adjusted to White House life; the children have gotten along well; I think it has brought our family closer together. Our children have matured very well in the White House. It's been helpful to them. I'm absolutely enthusiastic about the job." Would he be writing all this in a book some time? "I don't expect to for a few years," said Gerald Ford. ∎

PUTTIN' ON THE RITZ

The American President is both monarch and Prime Minister, serving not only as the nation's Chief Executive, but also as the foremost embodiment of our national heritage and aspirations. It's a balancing act, for Americans expect their Presidents to have the common touch—seasoned with a dash of royal display.

KENNEDY MAGIC

At a 1961 Inaugural Gala with Vice President Lyndon Johnson, John and Jacqueline Kennedy exude the glamour that became their hallmark.

AT THE END OF HIS ROPE

The scene: Dwight Eisenhower's first Inauguration, in 1953. Montie Montana, a cowboy who had appeared in many Western films, asked the new President's permission to encircle him with his lasso; receiving Ike's nod, he proceeded to get his man. Said Montie later: "I was lucky the Secret Service didn't ventilate me." History records that Thomas Jefferson simply walked from his Washington boarding house to the Senate chamber of the Capitol Building for his Inauguration in 1801. Since then, Inaugurals have become increasingly complex: today the actual swearing-in of the Chief Executive is the centerpiece of a days-long whirl of balls, dinners and concerts.

TOGA PARTY

Soon after taking office, Franklin D. Roosevelt was accused of attempting to reign as an "American Caesar." Rather than take umbrage at his critics, he retaliated by poking fun at them. To celebrate the President's 52nd birthday, in 1934, Roosevelt and a few intimate friends, a group known as the Cufflinks Club, dressed up as a Roman imperial court. A tickled Eleanor Roosevelt, as the Delphic Oracle, can be seen just behind her laurel-bedecked husband; daughter Anna and friends were Vestal Virgins. This picture of a private gathering, which could easily have been misconstrued, remained unpublished until 1973.

STRAIGHTENING UP

In September 1995, principals in the watershed Middle
East agreement to expand Palestinian self-rule on the
West Bank came to the White House for a signing session
(from left: Israel's Yitzhak Rabin, Egypt's Hosni Mubarak,
Jordan's King Hussein, President Clinton, P.L.O. Chair-
man Yasser Arafat). As the heads of state convened for the
ceremony, official White House photographer Barbara
Kinney caught this backstage view of history. Said Kinney:
"An aide said, 'Oh, Mr. Clinton, your tie's a little crooked,
you might want to fix that.' He did, and out of the corner
of my eye, I realized they were all doing it, out of instinct."
Sadly, Rabin was assassinated only five weeks later.

CUTTING IN

February 6, 1981, was a highly festive occasion for
Ronald and Nancy Reagan: they had moved into the
White House only weeks before, on a tide of national
emotion and relief—for the seemingly endless hostage
crisis with Iran had been resolved the day of Reagan's
Inauguration, when Ayatullah Khomeini ordered the
release of the American prisoners. The couple celebrated
Reagan's 70th birthday (he was the oldest President to
take office) with a gala affair involving dinner and
dancing with old friends, including Frank Sinatra—
who seems to be enjoying his twirl with the First Lady
a bit more than the President might like.

COMPANY!

As the most prominent exemplar of American culture, the President eventually gets around to gripping and grinning with many of the nation's celebrities.

Left, advocate for the disabled Helen Keller gets to know President Eisenhower in 1953.

Right, Elvis Presley came to Washington in December 1970 and sent a letter requesting a meeting with the President. When Nixon obliged, Presley told him he wanted to help fight drug abuse.

THRILLED

Left, Michael Jackson has a glove-in with George Bush in 1990.

Right, on tour in 1974, musicians Billy Preston, ex-Beatle George Harrison, Ravi Shankar and Tom Scott visit with Gerald Ford and his son Jack.

Above right, Bill Clinton chats with a lesbian couple, comic Ellen DeGeneres and actress Anne Heche, at the 1997 White House Correspondents Dinner. DeGeneres had just made news by declaring "Yep, I'm Gay" on TIME's cover.

A HOME FOR THE ARTS

John and Jacqueline Kennedy brought a new vision of the White House to the presidency: they believed the executive mansion should be a showplace for American art and culture. Their glittering evenings, featuring a scintillating mix of New York and Boston intellectuals, Hollywood stars, famous athletes—and the world's most acclaimed artists as after-dinner entertainment—became legendary, and every succeeding President has followed their example. Above, cellist Pablo Casals, 84, performs at a 1961 dinner; he had first appeared at the White House in the presidency of Teddy Roosevelt.

THAT '50s FEELING

Dwight Eisenhower, a veteran of many a chow line,
moves through an Inaugural buffet in 1953, followed by
Vice President Richard Nixon. Ike liked the good life; his
golfing and card-playing friends were drawn from the
upper echelons of American business life. His tastes were
exactly in synch with the decade he presided over from the
White House: the good life meant grilling steaks outdoors,
eating dinner on TV trays and driving massive new cars on
massive new highways. Eisenhower's strong advocacy of the
federal interstate highway system accelerated America's
transformation from an urban to a suburban culture.

AUTOGRAPH HOUND

John Kennedy gets Harry Truman's autograph on his program
at an Inaugural brunch, 1961. Though Truman had vigorously
opposed J.F.K. as the Democrats' nominee in 1960, he campaigned
for the young Senator once he won the nomination. The day after the
Inauguration, Truman visited the White House for the first time
since he had left it in 1953: he and Dwight Eisenhower had a very
frosty relationship, and Truman sometimes called the war hero
"Alibi Ike." After dinner, Kennedy had arranged a piano concert by
the virtuoso Eugene List, who had played for Truman at the Potsdam
Conference in 1945. At one point, Truman sat down at the keyboard
and played a Chopin polonaise. Truman was later disappointed that
Kennedy seldom sought his advice during his presidency.

PROUD PAPA

Bill and Hillary Rodham Clinton are one of the most controversial couples ever to occupy the White House, so much so that the term "Clinton hater" became shorthand for a presidential foe. But on one subject the Clintons' detractors and admirers agreed: their daughter Chelsea, 20 in 2000, is a bright, articulate young woman who has passed the ordeal of growing up in the public arena with flying colors. Vowing from their first days in the White House to protect Chelsea's privacy, the Clintons asked the media to restrict their coverage of her, and most U.S. news organizations have complied with the ad hoc embargo on the pre-med student's doings at Stanford University and elsewhere. Above, the President's opinion of his daughter is evident in a picture taken at an Inaugural Gala in 1997.

FIVE BIG GUNS

Aboard the battleship U.S.S.
Iowa in New York Harbor,
Ronald and Nancy Reagan
preside over the celebrations
honoring the restoration of
the Statue of Liberty in 1986.
The day's highlights included
a sail-in of tall ships from
around the world, a show of
U.S. military might, British
Harrier jets hovering in
mid-air and dipping their
noses to the statue, and the
mass swearing-in of hundreds
of immigrants as new citizens.
In short, it was the sort of red-
white-and-blue extravaganza
that was guaranteed to make
Reagan choke up.

Plains, Georgia, 1979

Jimmy Carter

Proud to be a Washington outsider, he treated the White House as a pulpit—but the results were not always bully

JIMMY AND ROSALYNN CARTER GOT OUT OF the presidential limousine below the Capitol after his Inauguration on a crisp January day in 1977 and walked hand in hand down Pennsylvania Avenue to their new home, the White House, all the way waving to the cheering crowds, the first time in memory that Washington had seen such a common touch.

The President was an outlander from far beyond the infamous Beltway and proud of it, determined to remain so. He was the man who had carried his own suit bag when he stormed the bastions of the old Democratic Party in the primaries. He stayed in the homes of working people, and he marshaled busloads of family and friends (the "Peanut Brigade") to pass on his message for a government "as good as the American people."

On that Inauguration Day, Carter admitted he was heady with the cheers of well-wishers, but his mother, Miz Lillian, a peppery and independent woman who had shaped her son in much the same mold as herself, was on hand for a reality check.

"On the way between the parade and the White House," Carter later related to me, "we were con-fronted with a whole array of TV cameras. Everybody wanted to talk to me." But press secretary Jody Powell had urged the family to avoid the questioners in those crowded and unguarded hours ready-made for embarrassing gaffes.

"Typically, my mother said, 'Jody, you can go to hell. I'll talk to whomever I wish.'" Carter remembered. "And the first question was, 'Miz Lillian, aren't you proud of your son?' I moved very close to hear my mama's complimentary response, and Mama said, 'Which one?' It kind of brought me down to earth even before I got to the White House."

Though he had served as Governor of Georgia in Atlanta, his heart was in Plains, the tiny town where the Carter family's peanut fields and warehouses were centered. From that vantage point Carter was convinced that the U.S. government had bogged down within itself, lost direction and heart.

There are some of us who watched Carter's one term slide into doubt and turmoil who believe that he was almost too idealistic for the job. He was a man of intense faith, a reborn Christian. The concerns of others came first in his mind. He did everything in his power to avoid hurting anyone. But in

had worked that miracle despite the bitter legacy of a generation of wars, nurturing the flame of peace through a year and a half of nitpicking negotiations and the final endless nights at Camp David when time and time again the two antagonists came close, only to reject an agreement.

The Carter who inspired this giant step toward peace was not the same one who had walked down Pennsylvania Avenue two years before. "If he'd only been this way earlier, he could have done so much more," lamented an aide. Carter himself seemed to sense his own new worldliness, forged by numbing work and seasoned by earlier disappointments. "Peace has come," he told friends and staff through the triumphant day. But always he added, "We have hard times ahead."

The Carters got out of the limousine and walked hand in hand to their new home, the first time in memory we had seen such a common touch

the presidency that can be a hindrance. Historian Arthur Schlesinger Jr. once wrote that every decision a President makes means that he honors one group but rejects the pleas of another, and almost always there is bitter protest. That was not a world Jimmy Carter enjoyed.

His deep compassion intruded into the grim tableau when 52 Americans were held hostage in the U.S. embassy in Tehran. The small things clouded his vision of the larger purpose. At one point in planning Desert One, the inadequate scheme to rescue the hostages that ended in tragic failure, Carter wondered about the Iranian guards stationed inside the embassy, near the wall the commando assault team would scale. Were they volunteers or conscripts? Carter asked the officers and aides gathered around him in the White House Situation Room. If they were hardened radicals, Carter said he could go along with killing them. But if they were only peasant conscripts, he wanted them knocked out temporarily, not killed.

One of Carter's aides who stood near the President told me later, "I knew at that moment, this rescue effort would fail." Carter suffered from what some historians have called "the tyranny of the trivial," by which preoccupation with unpleasant details destroys an inherently noble effort.

Yet that grasp of detail could pay huge dividends, under unusual circumstances. In twelve days of tortuous negotiations at Camp David, Carter, with his deep knowledge and understanding of the Middle East's history and ancient antagonisms, worked what even some of his critics called "a miracle" and produced a peace accord between Egypt's Anwar Sadat and Israel's Menachem Begin.

When Carter was able to summon hundreds of guests for the signing of the accord to the White House lawn, it was a remarkable tribute to his intelligence and sensitivity. He

Carter's presidential cupboard, though deeply troubled by high inflation and interest rates, was far from bare as he entered the re-election campaign in 1980. He had negotiated the new Panama Canal treaties, won some deregulation in the transportation industries, stood resolutely at home and abroad for human rights and completed the normalization of relations with China—a diverse and worthy record.

And the man's personal honesty and candor were undimmed. He was a marvelous friend and neighbor down at 1600 Pennsylvania Avenue. There was grace at every meal, prayer and Bible reading and even Sunday school in the balcony of the First Baptist Church down the street. There was Willie Nelson on the stereo, jogging in the back yard on cool summer mornings and iced tea with shoes off on the Truman balcony. There was a cardigan sweater, nicely worn at the edges, for the crisp fall days.

Jimmy Carter lost his bid for a second term. He was hammered by a slumping economy that he could not straighten out, and there was the sour taste from the American hostages still festering in the compound in Iran. Carter never complained or felt sorry for himself. While negotiating for the release of the hostages, he went without sleep for two nights before he passed the presidency to Ronald Reagan.

The new President could stand in the bright sun after taking his oath on the west Capitol lawn and announce the stunning news and proclaim it was morning in America. For the weary Carter seated at his side, it was the end of one dream but the beginning of another. As a former President, Carter has ministered across the globe to people who were ravaged by war and hunger and natural calamities. After leaving the White House he became in many ways a more admirable and influential figure on the world stage than he was while he lived there—an outlander to the last. ■

1931

PLAINS Jimmy Carter was born on October 1, 1924. His father Earl was a farmer in tiny Plains, Georgia; mother Lillian was a free-thinking nurse who took an active interest in the health of the local poor and blacks. While Earl's farm prospered, Jimmy worked hard, saved money and became a landlord at age 13, buying five houses he would own until 1949.

The Peanut Farmer

1937

1946

COUNTRY BOY Jimmy's uncle was a sailor whose travels, related by postcard, enthralled the youngster; he aimed for the U.S. Naval Academy before beginning high school. After high school, he worked on the farm and took classes at Georgia Tech until beginning studies at Annapolis in 1943.

ROSALYNN Carter graduated from the Naval Academy in 1946. He married Rosalynn Smith that summer; a junior in college, she was a local girl who had grown up near him in Plains. She turned down his first proposal then relented, eager to escape from small-town life. The Carters had four children.

1970

POLITICS After serving seven years in the Navy, Carter returned to Plains in 1953 to manage the family business after his father's death—to Rosalynn's disappointment. Taking an interest in local poli-tics, he headed the school board then served in the state senate. After a defeat in the Democratic gubernatorial primary in 1966, he staged a successful run for Governor in 1970, left.

1976

KINFOLK Carter was the first President to hail from the Deep South in more than a century. His feisty mom, who had joined the Peace Corps after age 60, and his brother Billy, a down-home good ole boy, took turns charming and alarming Americans.

Uncle Sam's Energy Crisis

Out of gas and running low on luck, Jimmy Carter's nation weathered four tough years

1979

1979

1979

TODAY the PANAMA CANAL TAIWAN TOMORROW!

MARYLAND LEGISLATURE SAYS "HANDS OFF OUR CANAL"

KEEP THE AMERICAN CANAL

Give 'em LANCE KEEP OUR CANAL

1977

1979

DRIFTING: Jimmy Carter strode into the presidency on a wave of hope. After more than a decade of war in Vietnam, riots in the cities and misdeeds in the Oval Office, Americans embraced the promise of a fresh face. But the four years of Carter's term proved difficult, as a plague of unexpected crises descended on the country.

In 1979 an accident at the nuclear power plant at Three Mile Island in Pennsylvania raised serious concerns about the future of nuclear energy. And when the Organization of Petroleum Exporting Countries radically increased the price of crude oil in 1979, Americans faced long lines at the gas pump (above), even as raging inflation put a further dent in their pocketbooks.

More crises exploded abroad: in 1978 Muslim fundamentalist Ayatullah Khomeini took power in Iran, and beginning in November 1979, radicals held 52 U.S. citizens hostage in Tehran (left). Carter's rescue mission in April 1980 turned into a fiasco in the desert. In July 1979 leftist Sandinistas ousted the corrupt rulers of Nicaragua, bringing the cold war to Central America. And in December 1979 Soviet troops invaded Afghanistan (far left), intent on turning it into a puppet nation.

There was good news during Carter's term, as well. He scored a personal triumph in 1977 by engineering congressional approval of the handover of the Panama Canal to Panama, though the action was condemned by many (left). In 1978 Karol Wojtyla, a Pole, was elected Pope: as John Paul II, he would help power the growing demand for freedom in Eastern Europe.

The Big Question: *Who* Carter?

GEORGIE   WOODY   HERBIE

To have a President named "Jimmy" took some getting used to, as you can see from this column in Carter's first year. He made it stick, being a man of independent mind. But I still wonder if he did not prejudice his presence in Washington in those early months in his Administration by insisting on that Southern folks' manner of identification.

SAY THIS SLOWLY: "PRESIDENT JAMES E. CARTER." Not bad, huh? But it drives the White House wild. What about this one: "President J. Earl Carter Jr.," or maybe just "President J.E. Carter"? Nope, says the White House, it has to be "Jimmy."

President Jimmy Carter has institutionalized his hypocorism with determination and skill, thus becoming the first President in history to get away with official use of a nickname. He is also the first to want to.

This historic breakthrough hit home last week when a handsome new book, *The Presidents,* by the National Park Service, was mailed around town. George, John, Thomas, Andrew, William, Millard, Abraham, Chester, Warren and all those others march formally out of history. There are other Jameses too, but with last names like Madison, Monroe and Polk. At the end is No. 39: Jimmy.

The historians at the Park Service had been a little uncomfortable about the jarring informality, but they checked with the White House. Back came the order: Jimmy. The Library of Congress has him down in the file of all card files as Jimmy. The *Encyclopaedia Britannica* gulped hard and dedicated its latest edition to "President Jimmy Carter and Her Majesty Queen Elizabeth II." The capital's *Social List* wanted to make it James Earl, but an alarmed member of Mrs. Carter's staff called up and said, "Absolutely not." It now reads, on page 120, "Carter, the President of the United States, and Mrs. Jimmy." The British Broadcasting Corporation had a policy meeting on the Jimmy issue. In broadcasting, particularly British broadcasting, Christian names stand like the Tower of London. But the BBC retreated. Whenever possible, British newscasters refer to President Carter. But now and then they must relent and say the nickname, and when they do, according to an American-language expert just back from London, Barnard's Professor Richard Norman, they look uncomfortable.

John Algeo, head of the English department at the University of Georgia, himself an onomastic authority, offers this theory: the Jimmy phenomenon is a bit of transplanted Southern tradition. He realizes some Yankees consider nicknames childish and undignified. There are more adult Jimmys and Billys in the South, noted Algeo, partly because there is less infant baptism than up North and nicknames are more likely to get started and stick before the ceremony intervenes. Some pollsters have suggested that the nickname helped Carter gain traction with younger voters. But as criticism of Carter has mounted, his seemingly casual, unorthodox approach to the presidency may now be working against him.

Nevertheless, Carter has been winning the name game for a decade in public life and is not about to give up. As Governor, he got a ruling from the Georgia secretary of state that he could legally use his nickname. In the presidential election, South Carolina and Maine balked at putting "Jimmy" on the ballot. Carter's lawyers successfully argued in court that "it was the actual name by which the public knows and recognizes him." Maine Superior Court Justice David Nichols wrote, "It appears that, without resorting to judicial proceedings, this nominee did change his name to Jimmy Carter. His change was in the pattern of such Presidents as were at birth named Hiram Ulysses Grant, Stephen Grover Cleveland, Thomas Woodrow Wilson and John Calvin Coolidge."

NBC commentator Edwin Newman, a language connoisseur, doesn't agree. Says he: "I don't like it [Jimmy], but he's entitled to use the name he wants ... I wonder if it would have helped if we had had 'Herbie Hoover' in the White House."

One institution is holding fast—Marquis Who's Who, Inc., has issued a new *Who's Who in Government,* and the entry on the 39th President comes under "Carter, James Earl, Jr." But on down, under "Carter, James Marshall" (a federal judge), is this line: "Carter, Jimmy—see James Earl, Jr. (Jimmy)." ■

In Celebration of Peace

Jimmy Carter was at his best when immersed in the details of policy and history and nations and not required to make instant decisions of life and death. When he could talk one on one with protagonists like Israel's Menachem Begin and Egypt's Anwar Sadat, Carter's openness and honesty carried the day. This Middle East breakthrough was a remarkable moment for the world—and for Jimmy Carter.

PEOPLE HAVE SWARMED OVER THE WHITE HOUSE lawns and stood along Pennsylvania Avenue in celebration, fear and anger. They have come to the mansion for Inaugurations and parades. They have wedded, buried, hunted Easter eggs and eaten barbecue, but not in 179 years had they gathered to witness a creative act of peace so full of promise for the future, although the risks were plain to see. Before 1,600 guests and another 5,000 spectators and a global TV audience of maybe a hundred million, two of the world's most implacable antagonists signed a formal treaty of peace and eloquently pledged their determination as men of God to heed the pleas of Isaiah to "beat their swords into plowshares, and their spears into pruning hooks."

In another setting, at a different time, last week's event might have seemed not only mawkish but mocking. But the urgency and simplicity of their message and the deep spiritual bond of the men generated a rare aura along old Pennsylvania Avenue. Egypt's Anwar Sadat, the secret hero of this city of monuments, stroked his name with his own pen. Israel's Menachem Begin, fierce fighter turned tough negotiator, created the ceremony's touch of humor by kidding himself as a legal nitpicker. He had his yarmulke, too, which he slipped on his head while he read the 126th Psalm in Hebrew ("They that sow in tears shall reap in joy"). Between these two old foes, warmed by a reluctant spring sun, sat President Jimmy Carter, etched and tired but aglow with the moment. He signed as a witness to this singular marriage of hope.

It was a time of filtered joy. The scars of four wars, the strain of 16 tortuous months of negotiations that went on to the last hour and continued even after the signing, the difficulties that everyone knows lie ahead, all were visible on the faces of the three participants. Sadat, who will be confronted now with increased threats to his safety and political subversion from radical Arabs, clearly sensed the hard battle coming and the fragile nature of the treaty they had signed. Begin relished the idea of pushing off on this "adventure of becoming fully human, neighbors, even brothers and sisters," to use the words of Carter. The U.S.

President was prayerful and cautious, too many times burned by his amateur exuberance, smart enough now not to believe dreams arrive on printed pages. "Peace has come," he said quietly, but he added again and again before the day was out: "We have no illusions."

There have been moments before along the national avenue when all hearts have joined and politics was left behind. When Ike rode down the street at the end of World War II, there were no Republicans or Democrats to be found—only Americans. And when John Kennedy announced that the Cuban missile crisis was resolved, the sigh of relief was audible throughout the federal city. The same sense of oneness crept over the North Lawn last week and engulfed the gathering. Zionist literally rubbed elbows with Arab. Men who had shot at one another in the wars shook hands.

Clark Clifford, 72, standing beneath one of the huge old elms planted in the time of Rutherford B. Hayes, thought of his own history in the President's office a few paces away. As Harry Truman's Counsellor, just 31 years ago this May, he had battled to win State Department backing for the recognition of the new nation to be formed in the Middle East; it came 11 minutes afterIsrael's birth. The Soviets came along some 70 hours later. Clifford understandably was a little misty-eyed on treaty morning. How long a journey it had been.

POWER LUNCH Before signing the landmark Camp David accord, the principals and their wives talked biblical history

Lunch was more social than businesslike. The three men and their wives dined modestly in the family quarters. Outside, the crowd was gathering and sounds filtered up through the tall windows. The three men began to talk history. The last time a treaty between the people of Israel and of Egypt had been signed, Begin said, was 3,000 years ago. King Solomon had made a deal with a Pharaoh. "I'll bet no one remembers the mediator," said Jimmy Carter. ∎

This Old House

America's memories and dreams find a home in the White House

THERE IS AN ENDURING VITALITY ABOUT THE WHITE House, and I feel it every time I go through the gate and up the drive. I always straighten up a bit, and my step quickens. Someplace along that drive 200 years ago, George Washington stood and surveyed the partially finished building. It took 10 years to build, but he was a determined man. The new Republic would have a suitable home for its President, even if he never would live there. He might be watching still—stand tall.

Today, after 43 years of reporting and writing about the people and events in and around the White House, I have a little chunk of history tucked away in my memory. When I returned from Dallas during that dark night on November 22, 1963, and wandered beneath the barren elms waiting for the return of John Kennedy's shattered body, about the only comfort lay in seeing that softly glowing façade and knowing it had seen such tragedy before. In quiet dignity, that old building embraced the young President one last time. On that night, at least, the White House to me was a living thing.

The White House is always ready for rituals of sympathy or celebrations of achievement. And its rites of passage from one President to another, whether unfolding by tragedy or in the

inexorable and lawful process of political succession, are its purpose. That night, even in the searing moment of violent death, not only of Kennedy but also of his New Frontier, the great stone building was in the process of renewal. Kennedy's office was being stripped and emptied and made ready for Lyndon Johnson. Some saw an imponderable cruelty in the grim transition. Others, schooled in history, knew that that was the genius of our system.

When Jimmy Carter filled the sun-brightened lawns with a joyous crowd to celebrate the signing of the Camp David peace accord, it would have been easy to forget reality. This was an important step in the search for peace between Arabs and Israelis. But that was a centuries-old conflict. I recall listening to the bells of St. John's Church from across Lafayette Park and being warmed by the soft murmur of the thousands who had come for the signing. And yet I remember glancing up at the White House and thinking that the building was telling us something: Be cautious; peace is a long and difficult process.

There was also the night when I glanced across the State Dining Room to watch George Bush, son of capitalism, and

Mikhail Gorbachev, the last heir to Soviet communism, joke and laugh and slap each other on the back while captains of America industry nodded approvingly. After evangelist Billy Graham called out to God to bless the whole unlikely gathering, from the foyer came the strains of the Marine Band, that institution born of war, now shaped for peace but forever a glorious reminder of struggles that were and those to come.

Always this singular center, which mixes family and power and tradition and change, has served as our tutor, teaching us that national government is an institution of people. History, like life, comes in increments. Maybe that's why I remember the evening walks with L.B.J. during the distressing years of the Vietnam War. He would bring along his beagles, Him and Her, and they would race over the South Lawn yipping at squirrels and stopping for a sniff at the base of the elm planted by John Quincy Adams in 1825. The shadows in Johnson's eyes would lighten for a time. Others who had walked there

PEACE CORPS: A happy crowd gathers for the signing of the landmark Camp David accord between Israel and Egypt in 1979

before him had borne terrible burdens. He was not alone. The Republic lived on. Indeed, the White House is judged by some as the world's most renowned building, perhaps its best-known symbol of liberty. On November 1, 2000, we will commemorate the 200th anniversary of its opening

Building and holding it were not an easy task. Early on, District of Columbia commissioners shut down a brothel operating among the shacks of the builders. Vehement protests produced one of the first capital compromises: the place was quietly reopened in another part of town.

Came the fateful day for the laying of the cornerstone—October 13, 1792—and the Freemasons formed up in Georgetown in proud regalia, marched down Pennsylvania Avenue, planted the stone and tucked in a small brass plaque noting the event. They repaired to the Fountain Inn and a sumptuous dinner with 32 toasts—and never bothered to document the location of the stone. The mystery remains, despite searches by radar, X rays and even dowsing rods. None of them could locate the stone.

But the President's House (it was not officially named the White House until 1902) went up. John Adams came down from Philadelphia in 1800 in a carriage with one manservant and pulled up to the front of the White House at noon, where a small crowd gathered from the muddy, raw neighborhood. He went inside, did a little business and went upstairs for supper, vowing he would soon move out. The mansion, then the biggest house in America, was too grand for his taste. Besides, it was not finished; in fact, it was barely habitable.

Its first decades were far from easy. The British burned out the building in 1814, and Confederate General Robert E. Lee constantly tried to capture it during the Civil War. There were proposals to enlarge the structure and make it a grand, European-style palace. Others wanted it moved to a more central location in the country. Mercifully, all such ideas died.

The White House was imbued with a great wish from the start. The irascible John Adams, on his second night in residence, writing a letter to his wife Abigail, must have felt the first stirrings of a powerful national destiny. "I pray heaven to bestow the best of blessings on this house and on all that shall hereafter inhabit it," he wrote. "May none but honest and wise men ever rule under this roof." Franklin Roosevelt had those words carved in the marble mantel of the State Dining Room 145 years later. They remain, in this tumultuous political year, the country's prayer. ■

Visions of the White House

The White House was designed by James Hoban, an Irish-American architect; its site was selected by George Washington, the only President never to live in it. The picture at top shows an addition to the building proposed in 1807 that would have added two porticoes; the plan was not adopted. The building was burned (above) in 1814 by British troops who captured Washington in the War of 1812. In 1861, during the Civil War (below), the building was guarded by Union troops. Second from bottom is a drawing of the building in 1877, during the presidency of Rutherford B. Hayes. By 1901 (bottom), large conservatories had been added to the side of building.

STARTING OVER: Machines took over (right) during the two-year renovation begun by Harry Truman in 1950. The historic rooms were removed in pieces numbered for rebuilding

Jersey City, New Jersey, 1980

Ronald W Reagan

A painter of visions from his early radio days, he often got the big picture right, even if he was fuzzy on the details

ABOUT THE TIME THE EXPERTS THINK THEY have figured out the secrets to presidential leadership, somebody comes along to upset all the tidy theories—somebody like Ronald Reagan.

What a résumé: graduate of Eureka College (known only to a few), sportscaster, grade-B movie actor, studio G.I. in World War II, labor union head, Governor of California. At the very least, one has to say it is an unusual mix of experiences on the way to the Oval Office, which tends to embrace Ivy Leaguers and lawyers.

It was even more exceptional to me, an Iowa child of the Depression. For I used to come home on scorching summer evenings in the mid-1930s after long hours in my father's print shop and turn on the old cathedral radio to pick up a little sports news as delivered by "Dutch" Reagan on station WHO over in Des Moines.

He was a sensation even then, and particularly in Iowa, which was not only locked in the Great Depression but also in a monstrous drought. There was not much joy around when the summer temperatures climbed over 100° and the dust storms blew out of the west in brown and orange billows that sifted down

open throats and through the tiniest window cracks. Dutch loved life and what he was doing, and you could hear it. I always felt a little better after a few bars of hope from Dutch. Indeed, it occurred to me that he just might be the only happy man in Iowa at the moment.

A half-century later, I walked into the Oval Office in the White House and there was President Ronald Reagan, and it occurred to me that he just might have been the only happy man right then in Washington, which is generally a despondent city, where if you wake up feeling good you seek out a doctor. Trouble is Washington's business.

I recall that day in 1981 clearly. Reagan had the same lopsided grin, had the same broad-shouldered, big-lapeled suits that seemed to come out of Hollywood; the familiar high, sleek pompadour combed from those heavy strands of dark hair, which he never dyed. Or did he? Nope. Milton Pitts, Reagan's barber for eight years, used to cut the President's hair about once every 10 days. He would steal a few of the cuttings, tuck them in a plastic bag and bring them to his shop, and we would inspect the hair for false coloring. One out of every hundred or so of Reagan's hairs, it turned out, was gray. No way could anyone dye a thatch in that manner.

The hair was symbolic: there was little that was fraudulent about Reagan. What you saw was the real man; what you heard was the real heart. He never claimed to be an academic genius, but he would not have traded his time at Eureka for a Harvard degree. He never knocked Iowa as a prairie compound for hicks. He rode horses, refereed Little League ball games, painted a vivid word picture of Big Ten football under crisp autumn skies and faked broadcasts of the Chicago Cubs from ticker accounts, a bit of accepted charlatanry in those days.

We were chortling once over those exploits when he told me a story about broadcasting the Drake Relays, a major track event in its day. He had moved to the side of the field with his microphone and all day long built suspense for the quarter-mile run. When the race occurred, a sponsor's message was still on the air. Reagan never faltered, though the

had Reagan. In a dramatic, nationally televised 1964 political speech in support of the conservative Barry Goldwater, Reagan condemned big, expensive and intrusive government. He said what millions of American were feeling and thinking, and he stepped up to a new level of celebrity.

When Reagan came to Washington, the world expected business as usual, particularly the leaders of the Soviet Union, who had always insisted there was no difference between Democrats and Republicans.

In the summer of his first year, the nation's air-traffic controllers went on strike, violating the terms of their federal employment. I went to the White House to hear Reagan's statement on the issue. In the Rose Garden, columnist Rowland Evans Jr. asked me what I thought would happen. The usual "study commission" for six months to delay a hard decision, I answered. Reagan came out from his office with his perpetual good cheer intact. He stepped up to the microphone and fired the controllers. I was stunned. The world was stunned too—and my friends at the CIA told me later that the secret cable traffic to communist regimes that night broke records. The gist: this President was different.

To this day, former British Prime Minister Margaret Thatcher credits Reagan for ending the cold war by building up U.S. military forces and by proposing, in the Strategic Defense Initiative, a program that the Soviets could not match, so that the Soviet Union was stretched to its economic limits trying to keep up. But Reagan had his woes. The Iran-*contra* affair, a fumbling attempt to fund pro-U.S. forces in Central America, went sour.

Reagan was shot and severely wounded by a young man in 1981, and he was bitterly derided when unemployment produced breadlines in 1982. Yet nothing seemed to dim his lus-

I used to come home on scorching summer evenings in Iowa and turn on the cathedral radio to catch a little sports news from "Dutch" Reagan in Des Moines. He loved life and what he was doing, and you could hear it

contest was finished. He had taken notes, and once back on the air he dramatized the completed sprint, hesitating only at the end when he realized there had been no cheers from the spectators. "Ladies and gentlemen," Reagan shouted into the mike, "the crowd has been stunned into silence!" When I stopped laughing, I said, "Mr. President, you were on your way to the White House right then."

Ronald Reagan changed Washington more than any modern President since Franklin Roosevelt, who created the Big Government that Reagan would attack. To a significant degree Reagan was cast up by the times in which he lived. He was a walking bit of history. His Roaring Twenties included a boozed-up father; he trudged the dreary streets of the Depression; he saw the rise of fascism in his morning paper; he studied World War II in the combat films he edited in Hollywood; he confronted the cold war and the social unrest of the 1960s and '70s as a public official.

By then the nation had pretty much concluded that government was often the problem, not the solution—and so

ter. Both the nation and Reagan recovered, and the "Great Communicator" was more beloved than ever. Reagan never abandoned his simple, forceful themes, never second-guessed himself, gave his genial message over and over. "You have to tell 'em what you're going to tell 'em," he explained. "Then you tell 'em. And finally, you tell 'em what you've told 'em."

He was never a detail man or even well tutored on many of the big issues. A lot of the pundits fretted he would be humiliated when he met the Soviet Union's brainy new boss, Mikhail Gorbachev, in Geneva in 1985. Instead it was plain that in the short summit meeting, Gorbachev had grown to like and respect Reagan. The two talked for hours about every imaginable subject, including Hollywood.

Later I got up the nerve to ask Reagan how he was able to stave off humiliation when the discussion turned to missiles and megatons, not a subject he had mastered in any form. Reagan looked at me and crinkled up. I had a sudden feeling we were back in Iowa and winging it. "Ah," he said. "Gorbachev didn't know any of that stuff either." ∎

1927

1928

1953

Leading Man

1979

1981

ILLINOIS BOY Ronald Reagan was born in the small town of Tampico, Illinois, on February 6, 1911. His father Jack was an Irish-American shoe salesman and a problem drinker. Reagan idolized his mother Nelle, who had a theatrical bent. "My father was a cynic and tended to suspect the worst of people; my mother was the opposite," he wrote. The family, including elder brother Neil, settled in Dixon, where Ronald, second from left, was a football star in high school.

LIFEGUARD For six years, Reagan was the sole lifeguard at Lowell Park on the Rock River north of Dixon; he is said to have saved 77 people from drowning. A good student, he was president of his high school.

ACTOR Reagan attended Eureka College in Eureka, Illinois, paying his own way and earning a football scholarship. At 21 he was hired as a sports announcer at radio station WOC in Davenport, which soon merged with the larger WHO in Des Moines; he became a local favorite. He left for Hollywood in 1937, after earning a six-month contract at Warner Bros. following a screen test.

STAR Reagan's first movie was *Love Is in the Air,* 1937. He married actress Jane Wyman in 1940; they divorced in 1949, after the birth of daughter Maureen and the adoption of son Michael. Reagan wed actress Nancy Davis in 1952; their children are Patti and Ron. Reagan became president of the Screen Actors Guild in 1947 and for 17 years was a General Electric spokesman.

POLITICS An F.D.R. fan who turned rightward, Reagan supported Barry Goldwater in 1964 and won the first of two terms as Governor of California in 1966. Defeated by Gerald Ford for the G.O.P. nod in 1976, Reagan beat Jimmy Carter in 1980. Left, he is wounded by a gunman after two months in office.

1987

1984

America on the Rebound

Ronald Reagan took a hard line against Soviet adventurism, with mixed results

1987

1983

TRANSITIONS: Few Presidents have come to power with such auspicious timing: on the day Ronald Reagan took the oath of office in 1981, Iran released the 52 U.S. hostages whose captivity had outraged Americans. Reagan's two terms saw the U.S. enjoy an economic recovery at home, following a recession in 1981-82, even as the demands for reform within the Soviet Union and its empire began to roil the Kremlin and bring the long cold war to its dénouement.

An avowed anticommunist and proponent of military might, Reagan bulked up the Pentagon budget and defied the U.S.S.R. by aiding anti-Soviet rebels in Afghanistan. But the bizarre Iran-*contra* scheme to fund rightist troops in Central America (top left center) by selling arms to Iran, run by Lieut. Colonel Oliver North, tarnished Reagan's last years. In 1982 Reagan sent U.S. Marines as part of a U.N. force to help calm religious strife in Lebanon, but the mission ended in disaster when a terrorist bomb killed 241 Marines (left).

At home, Reagan's right-wing appointees, like Secretary of the Interior James Watt, provoked howls of protest. When the AIDS crisis swelled in the early '80s, striking first among the gay community, Reagan was criticized for failing to respond. (Below left is the AIDS quilt.) And all Americans mourned in 1986, when the space shuttle *Challenger* exploded after lift-off and seven astronauts died.

1986

1981

WELCOME BACK TO FREEDOM

Leadership from the Heart

FACTUAL ERRORS IN SPEECHES WASH RIGHT OUT

REPELS BLAME FOR CENTRAL AMERICA TERRORISM

HOLDS SHAPE IN SPITE OF MIDEAST PEACE PLAN FIASCO

WON'T ABSORB CRITICISM OF ECONOMIC POLICIES FAVORING RICH

WRINKLE-FREE DESPITE DOMESTIC SPENDING CUTS

RESISTS BEIRUT BLOOD STAINS

SHEDS LINT AND $200 BILLION DEFICITS

DISPELS BLAME FOR APPOINTEES LIKE: WATT, CASEY, BURFORD, MEESE, ETC.

WON'T FADE DESPITE MASSIVE DEFENSE SPENDING

THE MAN IN THE TEFLON-COATED SUIT

NONSTICK MODEL Political cartoonist Paul Conrad skewers Reagan's legendary ability to ride out his political gaffes

Ronald Reagan's leadership was more of a mood than a box score, which was quite a change for those of us inside the Beltway, as this column attests.

RONALD REAGAN DEFIES TIDY SUMMARY. HE CANnot be measured by bills passed, treaties signed and doctrines proclaimed. Facts Reagan ain't. He is a refrain from *Stars and Stripes Forever.* He is a whiff of a kinder age out of the attic. He is reassurance, a pat on the back, a little belief in every person's dream. He is a do-ityourselfer in an era of easy cop-outs, a simple loyalist among the sophists, a gauzy visionary stumbling through computer printouts. He is comfort that things are not as bad as the experts say they are. Ronald Reagan is a mood that has seeped through the land like the beguiling scent of honeysuckle on a soft Georgia night. Millions have been soothed and seduced.

The political cognoscenti and academicians have been holding leadership seminars of late, and they thump their annotated treatises and bellow about "purposeful agendas" and "policy initiatives," and there is nothing that emerges from these deep encounters that looks or sounds like Ronald Reagan. Maybe it's time to rewrite the book of leadership.

The highest compliment comes from Democratic candidate Walter Mondale. He goes around saying, though not in so many words, that the broad themes of Reagan's presidency (less government at home, more strength abroad) are correct but that Reagan has executed them badly and often unfairly. Mondale is absolutely right. Reagan's kooky budget formula prolonged and deepened the recession and produced huge deficits. Reagan has had an unusual number of nincompoops working for his Administration. His insensitivities to the poor are monumental. His opposition to abortion and support for school prayer smack of zealotry. He still cannot comprehend the feminists. His beloved military wastes money hand over fist. But these are secondary issues. Those qualities of the spirit that Reagan so relentlessly thunders from the White House are what free and self-governing societies run on. It may yet be written in the history books that the genius of the Reagan years was to slow up the Federal Government, shrink the missionary ardor of the presidency and pep-talk America into doing a lot more for itself.

The U.S. government spends $2.3 billion a day and has so many departments, agencies and committees that a few years ago the experts quit counting after listing more than a thousand. Reagan has little notion how it all works but a lot of feeling that it is too big and too expensive and tries to do too much for too many people. Reagan believes a little neglect may be good for you.

The wise and witty Barber Conable, a 20-year Congressman from New York, espoused a form of Reaganism before Reagan came to Washington. "Government is not the system," says Conable. "The involved citizens of America do their own thing, bring about change and then drag government kicking and screaming into recognizing that change has occurred. Those who want a government that solves everybody's problems efficiently should turn to some other system. Liberal thinkers yearn for philosopherkings with the power and will to do for the people what the people are not yet ready for. It's safer to let the people decide first, even though it's not very inspiring to have a laggard government. The founding fathers didn't want efficient, adventurous governments, fearing they would intrude on our individual liberties. I think they were right."

So does Reagan. But if you asked him to talk about it at a Harvard seminar, he would have a terrible time. He would get his facts mixed up and tell a few stories that were wrong and lapse into some anecdotes from his movie days. There would not be much to quote, and there might be a lot to ridicule. But there would be no mistaking how he felt. That is Reagan's power. ∎

Reagan: "Let's Do It"

Whether on the budget, the striking air-traffic controllers or matters of U.S. defense, Ronald Reagan made decisions quickly and clearly and then rarely looked back to second-guess himself. He trusted others to carry out his orders. This action against terrorists was such a decision, and is one of many reasons why Reagan has now moved near the top of the list of successful Presidents, as measured by historians.

THE EDITORIAL IN THE WASHINGTON *TIMES* HIT HIM hard on that Thursday morning. FISH OR CUT BAIT, MR. REAGAN, read the headline. These were his conservative friends talking. "If Ronald Reagan again fails to avenge the death of a defenseless American, his constituents will want to know why they sent him back for a second term." Reagan brooded about it as he hurried through his morning briefing on the aftermath of the hijacking of the cruise ship *Achille Lauro* by pro-P.L.O. terrorists. Although U.S. intelligence had pinpointed the culprits in Egypt, and a scheme was being hatched to try and capture them if they fled, they were still out of reach.

Reagan's frustration was deep. He had been thwarted after the Marines and the U.S. embassy were bombed in Lebanon. Before he left the Oval Office for another flying tour to plug tax reform, he ordered National Security Adviser Robert McFarlane to use every intelligence source available to track the ship hijackers. Then he strode to his waiting helicopter. The editorial still rankled. As the chopper lifted off, Reagan protested to his aides: Did not his critics understand that to kill innocent bystanders would cast him as a terrorist? What he wanted, and what he would wait for, Reagan said, was "a clean one," the chance to strike directly at the guilty.

As his jet sped toward Chicago, events were unfolding that would give Reagan a clean one. But it is almost a given in the history of presidential leadership that nothing happens when it should. This caravan was a celebration for tax reform, with bands and balloons and healthy Americans cheering. The President had to wear two faces that day, one for his happy crowds in public, another for his private moments as terrorism avenger. The moment of truth came just after he had addressed the employees of the Sara Lee Bakery in Deerfield, Illinois. By any measure it is a singularly clear look at how Ronald Reagan decides, and that is the very essence of being President.

As he spoke to the enraptured employees of Sara Lee, the word was flashed to McFarlane about the terrorists' plans to fly out of Cairo. Onstage, Reagan thundered his ire against deficits and roared another pledge to get spending down. "God bless you," he shouted from behind his famous grin, and the crowd cheered. Behind the stage in an employee conference room, McFarlane and his aides waited somberly with their news. Reagan entered, the door closed, the men who run the U.S. huddled.

"Can we make sure it's them?" Reagan asked first. We could, came the answer. "What risk will there be to innocent persons?" was Reagan's next question. Not much. But what risk to the Americans carrying out the mission? And what would be the diplomatic costs? Reagan listened to the answers as the outside din began to fade.

Those gathered with the President watched his eyes, his face. There was no wrenching emotion. Something inside the man had hardened long ago, and now the pieces were being fitted into place. At last, a clean shot. Reagan's questions and the answers took just two minutes. A few more seconds ticked off. "Let's do it," he said evenly. In 25 minutes his orders were in the heads of F-14 pilots on the deck of the carrier *Saratoga* in the Mediterranean.

Rarely have the intelligence, diplomatic and military apparatuses of the U. S. been in such good shape. Perhaps that is one reason Reagan could move through this drama so effortlessly. He had faith in his system. He did not pick over the details of the intercept plan, as Jimmy Carter did for the ill-fated Desert One raid in Iran. He did not ask who was at the other end of the command line, as John

POSTMORTEM Israeli soldiers guard the *Achille Lauro* after the hijacking of the cruise ship, in which one American was killed

Kennedy did when he sent troops over the autobahn into West Berlin. Reagan trusted them all, right down to the nameless young men flying in their F-14s.

"The President never questioned whether we could do it or not," Secretary of Defense Caspar Weinberger said later. "He trusted us totally. And if it had not worked, he would not have blamed us. I've said it for a long time. He has better judgment than all the rest of us put together." ∎

DON'T ASK, DON'T TELL
Richard Nixon mastered chopsticks for his trip to China in 1972, but appears to need help identifying his entrée.

ON THE ROAD

Hit the road, Jack—and Ike and Jimmy. For many years Americans kept the world at a distance. But today U.S. Presidents act on a global stage. So bags must be packed—whether the itinerary is as inviting as a state dinner at Versailles or as daunting as a cold war showdown with a Soviet leader.

FOOTBALL DIPLOMACY

George Bush kicks back with his Japanese hosts, enjoying the traditional game of *kemari* on a 1992 state visit. Unfortunately for the President, the trip is more often remembered for his misfortune at a state dinner, when he briefly took sick. Bush admits to having a highly competitive streak; he claims even such generally sedate games as tiddlywinks are likely to turn into fierce contests when he faces friends or family. As President, he brought his love of horseshoes to the White House and had a pit installed; Bill Clinton had it removed.

MAN OF THE HOUR

Bill Clinton soaks up the local color on a visit to the small village
of Nayla, India, in March 2000. Clinton came into office pledging
to devote himself to a domestic agenda, but he has become the most
traveled President in history. His trips abroad have included summit
meetings, trade missions, visits with U.S. troops stationed in the
Balkans and numerous peace missions, including this one to the
subcontinent, where a nuclear arms race between bitter foes India
and Pakistan aroused heightened fears of war in the late '90s.

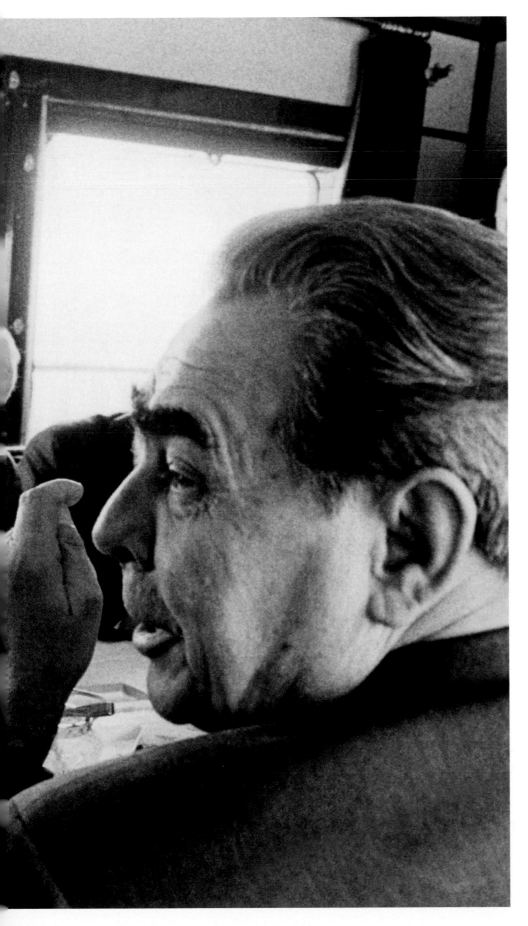

FACE TIME

In November 1974, Gerald Ford—thrust into office only three months before—traveled to Vladivostok on Russia's Pacific coast to lock eyes with Soviet Premier Leonid Brezhnev and discuss limiting the numbers of offensive nuclear weapons. In this picture, they are deep in talks on Brezhnev's train car. When Air Force One landed, Ford's mind was on more immediate matters than nuclear war: keenly aware that the Ohio State–Michigan football game was being played that day, the former Wolverine great immediately asked reporters, "What's the score?"

During the talks, Brezhnev admired a wolfskin coat that had been presented to Ford by U.S. military brass at a refueling stop in Alaska. Ford insisted the Russian take the jacket. Later, Ford told Hugh Sidey, Brezhnev took his hand in a private moment and urged the President to work with him to bring peace to the world— a rare instance when a Soviet strongman played a sheep in wolf's clothing.

ECHOES OF BATTLE

Ronald and Nancy Reagan journeyed to France in June 1984 to
mark the 40 anniversary of D-day. They joined 4,000 U.S. veterans of
the invasion and 6,000 other guests at Utah Beach as French President
François Mitterrand saluted the 10,000 Allied soldiers who had lost
their lives in the invasion. At nearby Pointe du Hoc, the Reagans
visited a German bunker, above. Hailing the 62 U.S. Rangers present
who had been among those who scaled the German-held promontory
over the English Channel, Reagan said, "These are the champions who
helped free a continent." Some of the veterans being congratulated for
their toughness had to take off their glasses to wipe away tears.

A TIME TO REMEMBER

In late December 1978 Jimmy Carter embarked on a nine-day, 18,500-mile odyssey, visiting Poland, Iran, India, Saudi Arabia, Egypt, France and Belgium. The highlights of the trip were a series of symbolic acts intended to emphasize his concern for human rights and global diversity. His first stop was Poland: when he placed a wreath at the Tomb of Poland's Unknown Soldier, more than 500 people broke through police lines, shouting, "Car-ter—Car-ter!" Later, when he placed flowers at the monument to the Jews who died in the 1943 uprising against the Nazis in the Warsaw ghetto, above, police kept away all but a handful of observers. Poland's communist government had tried to prevent the President from visiting both sites.

SADDLE TRAMPS

Left, Ronald Reagan and Queen Elizabeth II enjoy an outing at Windsor Castle in 1982. The two shared a love of horses—and gossip. Their quid pro quo: Reagan dished Hollywood dirt to the Queen, a movie buff, while she filled Reagan in on royal doings. Reagan loved to tell the story of the time he was host to the Queen at a state dinner. "Your Majesty, you should be over there," he pointed. "Yes, I know," she replied, "but you're standing on my gown."

JOHN F. WHO?

Right, Jackie Kennedy commands Charles de Gaulle's attention at a gala reception at Versailles during a state visit in June 1961. The wallflower languishing behind her famously described himself as "the man who accompanied Jacqueline Kennedy to Paris," for the French were bowled over by the First Lady's style, grace and way with their language. As Hugh Sidey recalls, "With its fountains illuminated and thousands of lights twinkling in the trees, Versailles looked like a fairyland. I was chatting with Letitia Baldrige, Mrs. Kennedy's social secretary, and we agreed: Jackie just might get to like her new job after all."

Saudi Arabia, 1990

George Bush

He sought to make America kinder and gentler, but he enjoyed his greatest triumph as Commander in Chief

GEORGE BUSH RAN THE GOVERNMENT BETTER than any other of the modern Presidents. None of them had the range of experience, none had the network of friends in the highest places around the globe, none collected a more talented and harmonious group of cabinet officers and aides than George Bush.

But Bush was uncomfortable with the new, raucous, self-trumpeting show-business world of elective politics, and it showed: he was cut short with a single term. His easy movements across the top rungs of power and his self-effacing manner left the perception that he did not fully comprehend the everyday anguishes of the American people, who often had more debts than money, frequent job worries and, always, health concerns. Maybe the nation was tired of Republicans after eight years of Ronald Reagan and four Bush years. Or maybe America wanted to change generations and looked to the "boomers" for a new leader. But there still is something of a mystery about why an administrator of such character and competence was rejected.

Hear Bush when he talked to me 100 days into his presidency and we were sitting outside the Oval Office in the spring sun: "I do hope that history will say that we helped make things a little kinder and gentler, helped keep the government from being anything other than a servant of the people, helped keep the peace."

That was a modest agenda. He lived up to it and then some. The cold war ended on his watch, and Bush wisely refused to gloat in public or shake his fist at the Soviet Union, struggling to right itself after the old regime had passed. "I am not going to manhandle the Soviet account," he told me one day before he set out on a journey through Europe to try to coax the new leaders to his side.

In Poland he listened to General Wojciech Jaruzelski, the communist boss who was on his way out, and Bush leaned over after the speech and patted his arm, a man in sympathy and not in vengeance. Next day he wrapped his arms around Solidarity leader Lech Walesa, the man who led the opposition to the communists and would become Poland's President.

A few months later, Bush was on the U.S. cruiser *Belknap* wallowing in heavy seas off Malta, waiting for 60-m.p.h. winds to subside so he could hold his first summit with Mikhail Gorbachev, the Soviet leader who would bring the disintegrating empire into the modern world. He had wanted a "feet on the table" meeting, Bush said before he left the U.S.

"Actually, I really did put my feet up at one point," he told me in a phone call after the summit. "I did it thinking, I'll show 'em I really did mean it to be a feet-up meeting. So I put my feet up on one of those round sofas. There were no inhibitions."

Whether or not it was this unique approach to diplomacy that sealed a friendship that goes on today, the President seemed to find a kindred spirit in the search for world peace. "I think I can trust Gorbachev," Bush told me. "I looked him in the eye. I appraised him. There was a twinkle. He has got a political feel. He has a wonderful way of communicating with Westerners."

ment if U.S. calculations were wrong and others feared a flood of body bags might return from the desert front.

When the members of Bush's team, which included Secretary of State James Baker, Secretary of Defense Dick Cheney and Chairman of the Joint Chiefs of Staff General Colin Powell, were not meeting with him, they were constantly on the phone with him ("I like to use this," Bush once said, tapping one of dozens of phones surrounding him). Bush's style was informal but insistent.

I recall in 1990 going to the White House for one of the Bush-family Christmas parties. The planning for Desert Storm was going on behind the scenes, but a visitor would not know that, because Bush wanted family and guests to be happily invested with Yuletide spirit. The gracious President rumbled Christmas carols; took the kids down into the White House basement to see the family dog, Millie; joked with the hired Santa Claus about his flowing beard.

As I was getting my coat after the party, I looked down a long, shadowy corridor and there was a file of men in sweaters and open shirts going quietly upstairs. They were Bush's command team for the war. I knew instantly that some major decision was in the works. Indeed, I found out later that on that festive day, Bush had dramatically shifted gears just as soon as Santa and the other guests left the White House. He set the dates for the coming desert battles in the air and on the ground.

In Poland, after the speech by General Jaruzelski, the communist boss on his way out, Bush patted his arm in sympathy and not in vengeance. Next day, he wrapped his arms around Solidarity leader Lech Walesa

Bush kept two bronze figures of Theodore Roosevelt around him in the Oval Office, which may help explain his belief in speaking softly but carrying a big stick. He successfully sent American forces into Panama in a miniature war to depose President Manuel Noriega, a drug dealer and plunderer of the public till. But when the Berlin Wall fell, in one of the great dramas of our time, Bush refused entreaties to fly to Berlin and stand on the collapsed wall and cast his scorn toward the Kremlin.

When Iraq's Saddam Hussein invaded and captured Kuwait, threatening the world's oil supply, Bush did not hesitate. He instantly "drew a line in the sand," stating that Saddam's forces would be thrown out of Kuwait. For the next few months, massive U.S. forces were assembled in the Middle East, and in 1991 Operation Desert Storm was unleashed, bringing a quick, stunning victory to America and her allies. It was Bush at his best, persuading the public, the Congress, the United Nations and the Arab alliance to join in the crusade, even as some critics threatened impeach-

A year after that remarkable victory in the Persian Gulf, Bush mused about the course of events while speaking to me. "I realized that Saddam felt we were bluffing. He was still living back in the Vietnam days. He didn't know we had a different ball game on here, different levels of technology, a different military force, a different President."

Bush ended the ground component of Desert Storm after 100 hours, as soon as Saddam's inept army was defeated and thrown out of Kuwait, retreating back across the Iraqi border in wreckage and turmoil. Criticism would dog the President because he did not go farther into Iraq, destroying more of its forces in the north and hunting down Saddam himself.

I had and still hold a different view. I had spent much of my professional life in Washington writing about wars of one kind or another that never seemed to end—the cold war, and wars in Korea, Central America and Vietnam. Bush had set his objective in Kuwait and achieved it brilliantly. He refused to enlarge and prolong the war, an act that took more courage than launching Desert Storm. ■

1930

1942

1945

1957

Born to Run

1983

BOYHOOD George Bush was born in Milton, Massachusetts, on June 12, 1924, second son in a family of five children; his father Prescott was a well-to-do investment banker who was elected a Senator from Connecticut in 1952. Mother Dorothy was born in Kennebunkport, Maine, which became a second home to the family. Groomed for success (he's sporting a tie at age 6), George attended the élite Phillips Academy, in Andover, Massachusetts.

SOLDIER, SCHOLAR At Andover, George (far left, bottom row) was a popular baseball player. Graduating in 1942, he enlisted in the Navy on his 18th birthday. He trained as a pilot; in 1944 his plane was shot down in the South Pacific, but he survived. After the war he went to Yale University, where he was captain of the baseball team. He graduated from Yale in 1948.

MARRIAGE George met Barbara Pierce before joining the Navy; her father was a magazine publisher. They married in 1945 and had six children; daughter Robin died of leukemia at age 3 in 1953.

OILMAN Bent on making his own way in the world, Bush went to Midland, Texas, in the postwar oil-rush days, where he worked for a large firm before co-founding his own company, Zapata, in 1953. At left, son George W. helps christen a rig in 1957.

DYNASTY Following in his father's footsteps, Bush ran for the Senate in 1964 but lost; in 1966 he was elected to the House from Texas' 7th District. He lost a second Senate race in 1970, but was named U.S. ambassador to the U.N., then U.S. liaison to China. In 1976 he became head of the CIA; in 1980 he was elected Vice President. After his term as President, he has seen sons George W. and Jeb maintain the Bush political tradition.

1992

Birth Pains of a New World

As the Berlin Wall and the U.S.S.R. crumbled, George Bush oversaw an age of change

1989

1989

1991

1990

1991

EVOLUTION: George Bush presided over a period of radical change in geopolitics from which the U.S. emerged as the globe's single remaining superpower. During his one term the cold war ended when the Soviet Union and its empire crumbled. The dramatic push toward freedom in Eastern Europe, initially sparked by the Solidarity movement in Poland, led by Lech Walesa, crested in the toppling of the Berlin Wall in November 1989 (below left). By 1990's end, pro-Soviet leaders had been ousted in Hungary, Poland, Czechoslovakia and even Romania; finally, in late December 1991 the Soviet Union itself dissolved.

In South Africa, the release of longtime political prisoner Nelson Mandela presaged the end of apartheid and the arrival of equal rights for blacks. Meanwhile, in forging his anti-Iraq Desert Storm alliance that united such disparate partners as Russia, the U.S. and Syria, Bush began to lay the framework for his new world order. Only in China was the tide of freedom held back, when government tanks crushed pro-democracy crowds in Beijing's Tiananmen Square in June 1989.

At home, Bush's Supreme Court nominee, Clarence Thomas, was accused of sexual harassment by former aide Anita Hill (above) in 1991. The congressional hearings gripped Americans and made sexual politics in the workplace a major issue of the 1990s. In 1992 racial unrest rocked Los Angeles (top left), when four policemen who had been captured on video brutalizing a black man, Rodney King, were acquitted by a mainly white jury.

Hitting the Right Chords

OLD PROS George Bush laughs with Roger Ailes, left, at the 1992 G.O.P. Convention

We keep trying to figure out fancy formulas for leadership. I must have a shelf of books 20 ft. long, all suggesting that the real answers lie within their covers. But so many variables reside within the heart of successful leadership as to baffle the most learned of scholars. In this early period of George Bush's presidency, he seemed to have the magic touch and appeared to be politically invulnerable. Perhaps he was. But the world changed, as it always does.

ROGER AILES, THE IMPRESARIO OF GEORGE BUSH'S triumphant run for the presidency, appeared on television the other day. There arrived shortly a note from the White House: "You were not bad, but your eye contact wasn't great. George."

The pupil has become the teacher, the tentative has become the confident. Or, to use another Ailes line, "George Bush has realized he does not have to audition anymore; he's got the job."

There are many people around Washington these days who say Bush actually looks different. One of his principal aides claims that three or four times recently, when discussing highly charged issues like the upheavals in China, Bush has cooled his own emotions with the line, "I'm the President now." There is little question that this realization can change a man's manner and mien.

Some national polls reflect a dramatic jump in approval. Gallup has Bush at 70%, up 14 points since May,

10 points higher than Ronald Reagan when he approached the six-month mark. A TIME/CNN poll taken last Wednesday shows Bush cruising along with 63% approval at a point when the presidential honeymoon generally comes to an end and a slide begins. Pundits have called this a "second honeymoon" and "Teflon II." Neither label seems quite right, since we now know that Bush takes showers with his dog—hardly the stuff of romance.

The President has won praise from such diverse people as Al Haig, a presidential contender who last year could not contain his contempt for Bush and Cyrus Vance and Ed Muskie, both Secretaries of State for Jimmy Carter. "Our differences are minimal," confesses James Schlesinger, the clear-eyed Cabinet officer fired for candor by both Jerry Ford and Jimmy Carter.

Even if it's too early to tell how his proposals will work, Bush's restraint and reason in arriving at most decisions seem to count for a lot. It could also be that Bush's very commonness is his virtuosity—common decency, common courtesy, common interests and common sense. Before he sat down last week to talk nukes with Australia's Prime Minister Bob Hawke, the President hacked around the scruffy Andrews Air Force Base golf course in suffocating heat. True, he had enjoyed roast saddle of veal at the state dinner, but by Wednesday he was off in Baltimore, downing a hot dog, some Maryland crab cakes and vanilla ice cream with his grandson, George P., 10, while the Orioles squeezed by the Toronto Blue Jays, 2-1.

Bush has touched every stratum of leadership in American society. Former Urban League president Vernon Jordan and IBM's chairman John Akers huddled with him. Country singer Crystal Gale and Alabama fishing guide Ray Scott were houseguests; Scott was sighted next morning in fatigues, appraising the South Lawn's fountains and pool. Previous Presidents have had profiles jagged with talents and flaws. Bush seems not to have those striking peaks and valleys.

When Ailes was asked to help get Bush elected, he applied his paramount rule for taking a job. "The candidate can't be nuts." Ailes figured then and figures today that he found a man cast in the concrete of sanity. ■

Tidings of Sadness and Loss

How deep the hurt from his defeat in 1992, few if any people knew. George Bush's whole life was shaped by self-discipline; his was a family that served but did not complain. Yet Bush had another life, and in short order he was jetting around the world giving speeches and dropping in on old friends still in power. Meantime, his sons George W. and Jeb were preparing their political careers amid talk of an approaching Bush family dynasty.

GEORGE BUSH WAS SHAPED AND TEMPERED BY HIS mother's nature. His was a soul finally formed by strata of love and discipline relentlessly laid down. Bush was lucky, so very lucky, to be rooted in a woman like Dorothy Walker Bush, who died last week at 91. But her death is added anguish in the President's season of political rejection, a burden few men have known. His steady goodwill in handing the White House over to Bill Clinton is a measure of a mother's implanted strength and a final tribute from a son. For Dorothy Bush was of another era, and her sense of propriety and modesty and self-control was cast in iron. That armored her second son for the rough reaches of politics. Hindered him too, in a fuzzy and formless era of national debate.

Oh, yes, son George strayed from the Dorothy doctrine: he began to talk about his virtuosities and his great record, but he was never comfortable doing it. He had the angel of that remarkable woman hovering over him. And his father, a stately tower of a man who used to walk the Senate chamber with mirth on his lips and a deep love of country. So much of George Bush is family.

So when George entered the killing field of presidential politics, he gave it a good amateur's try, but he never went the full distance. Here and there Bush has muttered a phrase or two about the transience of political power and wondering what is left when it passes. He has answered his own question. What is left is the infinite tenderness and love within a caring family. He had the best. And there is irony in the fact that he may never have understood that so many others were not so blessed by Providence, and that is one of the reasons he lost this election.

It is fascinating how these men who climb to the heights of power almost always at some point pause and look back and understand what they owe their mothers. There was a night in the long past when John Kennedy, so heralded as a son of the grasping, determined Joe Kennedy, lowered his voice and mused how his sense of history and understanding of this nation began with his mother Rose, not his father. "She was the one who told us about the founding fathers, who read history to us, who took us to Plymouth Rock and the Old North Church," he said.

Almost anytime, anywhere, Lyndon Johnson would tell you about Rebekah Baines Johnson, who pounded it into him that his way out of the hard life on the Texas plains was through education. Along the Pedernales River on the old family ranch one night when the moon was rising, he recalled to a friend the terrible times his mother went through trying to hold her family together and keep her dignity while living on the edge of poverty and uncertainty. She broke into tears one evening at the water pump, nearly overwhelmed with fatigue. Johnson, a small boy, put his arms around her legs and said he would take care of her. He always did. And she cared for him through that ethereal bond of motherhood.

It was the idea of obligation to others, as preached by Dorothy Bush, that drove the President into a life of service, now winding down in bittersweet days. His presidential record was better than anybody in this dismal campaign ever admitted, and better than he could articulate. And there was something more that could never be

INSIDER Dorothy Bush was no stranger to Washington politics; her husband Prescott had been a Senator from Connecticut

fitted into the strictures of raucous electronic politics: the sheer decency of the son of Prescott and Dorothy Bush.

All last week as his mother faded from this world, Bush toasted his friends and adversaries in elegant farewells. There was one night, after the ceremony ended, when there was a glimpse of the 41st President of this enduring republic standing in the corner of the mansion: he was sending Republicans and Democrats off into the night with one of his atrocious neckties flapping and his crooked grin playing across his face and his basic goodness asserting itself above all hurt and pain. History will remember. ∎

THE HELL WITH PRUDENCE

In March 1997, George Bush—age 72 and four years out of the White House—wowed Americans when he donned what he called an "Elvis suit" and joined members of the Army's élite Golden Knights on a parachute jump from 12,500 ft.

CURTAIN CALL

Free at last! Many Presidents might agree with
James Buchanan, who handed the White House over
to Abraham Lincoln with this optimistic sentiment:
"If you are as happy, my dear sir, on entering this
house as I am in leaving it and returning home, you
are the happiest man in the country."

FIT AS A FIDDLE

In retirement in Independence, Missouri, Harry Truman continued
to enjoy a morning constitutional—and often drew a crowd, as in this 1954
picture. Biographer David McCullough reported that in his later years,
Truman would often pause on his walk to speak to an enormous, aged
ginkgo tree. The former President also wrote his memoirs and delighted in
the Truman Library, where he worked daily: the oft-repeated remark was
that the most interesting item on display at the library was Truman himself.
After his death at 88 in 1972, his wife Bess ruled out plans for an elaborate
five-day state funeral that Truman had personally approved ("A damn fine
show. I just hate that I'm not going to be around to see it"). Mrs. Truman
("the boss," he had often called her) oversaw a shorter, simpler ceremony.

BUILDING A NEW LIFE

Since leaving the White House, Jimmy Carter has been an active
volunteer for the Habitat for Humanity, a charitable group that constructs
housing with and for the needy—here he's helping roof a home in Charlotte,
North Carolina, in 1987. Not content with simply overseeing the residue
of his White House years at his presidential library in Atlanta, he founded
the bustling, non-profit Carter Center to support his many ongoing activities.
In "retirement," Carter has circled the globe as a mediator in disputes,
as a special emissary for the U.S., as an election monitor and as a proponent
of better health and agriculture for citizens of the Third World. Carter,
who will turn 76 in 2000, now seems to enjoy the admiration of most
Americans, a goal that eluded him during his term in office.

CURTAIN CALL

BEACHED

Assessing Richard Nixon in August 1975, TIME ran this picture of him walking the beach alone at his San Clemente, California, home and reported, "One year after the fall, Nixon remains wan and drawn. At age 62, he tires easily and goes to bed early. In his thoughts, he often indulges in moments of self-pity. He feels he has been deserted by many of his one-time friends. He considers himself Watergate's wronged victim rather than its chief villain. He blames the media, his political enemies and bad advice from former aides for his unique role in American history as the only U.S. President ever forced to quit. Yet Nixon is neither continually depressed nor a beaten man. He is determined to regain his health and vindicate his presidency."

Nixon may not have succeeded in vindicating his presidency, but he regained his health, summoned his tireless spirit, moved to New York City and then New Jersey and reinvented himself as a valued elder statesman whose counsel was sought by many—including Bill Clinton. When the deeply complex former President died in 1994, TIME titled its obituary with a quote from Nixon that both his admirers and his detractors could not dispute: "I have never been a quitter."

FAREWELL

Sadly, Presidents Franklin D. Roosevelt and John F. Kennedy did not live to enjoy
a curtain call. Above, a citizen of Washington salutes the caisson bearing the body
of Roosevelt; his coffin had traveled by train from Warm Springs, Georgia, where
he died on April 12, 1945. Eighty years before, also in April, Washingtonians had
turned out to mourn another President who had brought the nation through war,
only to die with peace at hand, Abraham Lincoln. TIME's account of the Roosevelt
funeral procession: "Men stood bareheaded. Few people wept, so that the occasional
sounds of sobbing seemed shockingly loud. As the coffin went past, part of the
crowd began jostling quietly to move along, to keep it in sight. On Pennsylvania
Avenue an elderly weeping Negro woman sat on the curb, rocking and crying,
'Oh, he's gone. He's gone forever. I loved him so. He's never coming back.' "

"I READ THE NEWS TODAY, OH BOY"

The assassination of John F. Kennedy was shocking because he was such a young man—at only 46, he was admired, even affectionately mocked, for his "vigah." TIME's account of how the news spread: "Over Nob Hill and the Harvard Yard, across Washington's broad avenues and Pittsburgh's thrusting chimneys, in a thousand towns and villages the bells began to toll. In Caracas, Venezuela, a lone Marine sergeant strode across the lawn of the U.S. embassy while a soft rain fell, saluted the flag, then lowered it to half-staff. At U.S. bases from Korea to Germany artillery pieces boomed out every half-hour from dawn to dusk in a stately, protracted tattoo of grief." And on this New York City commuter train, businessmen took refuge behind their newspapers.

CURTAIN CALL

HAIL AND FAREWELL

Ronald Reagan waves goodbye to the capital from a presidential helicopter immediately after the Inauguration of George Bush in 1989. Reagan's retirement has been tinged with sadness. Once the embodiment of vigorous old age, he had seemed invincible: he had survived falls off horses, colon and skin cancers, prostate problems, even a bullet in the chest. But he shocked Americans in 1994 when he announced in a handwritten note to the nation that he was suffering from Alzheimer's disease. Health officials applauded his candor, saying it would help build awareness of a dread malady. Reagan lives in seclusion: his 89th birthday celebration, in February 2000, was limited to his family.

ONE FINAL CHORE

Dwight Eisenhower enjoyed a retirement befitting Cincinnatus, the Roman statesman-general. Ike moved to his farm in history-saturated Gettysburg, Pennsylvania, where he presided over 190 acres, with nine hands working his herd of more than 30 Aberdeen Angus cattle. He got around the place in a golf cart and faced only one major problem: tourists. In the time it took Ike to close a gate on the farm, LIFE magazine reported in the spring of 1961, five cars filled with vacationers stopped and soon they "were running at him with cameras and autograph books." Unfortunately, Eisenhower would not savor many years of tranquillity; he died in 1969 at age 78, eight years after leaving office.

Washington, 1994

William Jefferson Clinton

Impeached but not convicted, he was a brilliant, slick survivor who shed his liberal skin and balanced the budget

BILL CLINTON'S SURVIVAL AND MODEST POLICY successes in eight years of the presidency, during which time he was beset by constant charges of personal scandal that culminated in his impeachment and bitterly contested exoneration, are a modern political miracle and a testament to his understanding of the society of his time.

He came to power over George Bush in 1993 despite the accusations that he had dodged the Vietnam draft as a student and had had a not-so-secret affair with Little Rock torch singer Gennifer Flowers. In fact, it was rumored that that was one of many such affairs he had conducted while he was Governor of Arkansas and married to Hillary Rodham Clinton, father of Chelsea.

But Clinton could talk the talk even if he failed to walk the walk. He was dubbed "the comeback kid" at every turn when his personal flaws seemed to doom his career, for he, to use his words, "just kept getting up, just kept coming back." He was also "the man from Hope," a small-town boy who had risen to the heights of power on his intellect, his easy style and a lot of "friends of Bill" he had picked up along his lengthy academic journey through Georgetown Uni-

versity, Oxford (as a Rhodes scholar) and Yale, followed by 12 years in the Arkansas statehouse.

He was a shameless historical pirate, claiming at one time or another some kind of intellectual kinship with Lincoln, the two Roosevelts, Truman and Kennedy. For his Inaugural, he and his happy party boarded buses at Thomas Jefferson's Monticello and, presumably in the ghostly hands of the author of the Declaration of Independence, made their way to power in Washington.

The first two years of Clinton's leadership were some of the worst of this century. There was scandal in his Cabinet and within his White House staff, and his grand scheme for health-care reform, which he had put under his wife's supervision, failed in Congress, where it was perceived as a wildly expensive and unworkable proposal that would have created a host of new offices and bureaus, the ultimate nightmare of red tape.

The Republicans gained control of Congress in 1994, a shocking rebuke to the stumbling efforts of the Clinton Administration, though Clinton himself continued to remain personally popular with voters. His virtue seemed to be that he got out of the way of a surging private sector. Every President comes into office believing he will be a "heroic" President, one in the mold of Franklin Roosevelt, who fought economic depression and a great war. It was not to be for Clinton. To back away at times like this takes wisdom and no little courage. It is so much easier to be President in moments of crisis.

With the U.S. economy humming along and the cold war over, Clinton moved to the center of the political spectrum, declaring "the era of Big Government is over." He began to sound more like the early Ronald Reagan than the early Bill Clinton, who had been filled with ideas for government programs like those of the New Deal. He had run into the reality of this country, which didn't resemble the theories he had learned in his élite schools. The new Clinton championed balanced budgets and hailed the advent of the information age.

House intern, Monica Lewinsky. It was everything that the Clinton detractors had ever imagined or heard in the endless rush of rumors that followed him. She had given Clinton oral sex in and around the Oval Office, a fact that at first the President denied. Indeed, the larger disgrace of the episode, which more than anything else may have led to his impeachment, was a thoroughly plotted and rehearsed gambit for television in which Clinton wagged his finger at the American people and lied, "I did not have sexual relations with that woman."

Trapped by a cascade of contrary testimony, and pursued by a relentless independent counsel, Clinton finally admitted his error and his deviousness about it, and he sought counseling for his sexual problems. Hillary Rodham Clinton, while standing by the President in public, admitted privately it was a particularly trying time in a marriage that had always seemed to be on a roller coaster.

Still, they were a practiced couple on the presidential stage, disgraced or not. At the time when the news of the Lewinsky scandal broke, I sat a few yards away from the First Couple at a dinner for donors to the White House Endowment Fund, a pool of cash used to refurbish and polish the White House. They held hands; they looked tenderly into each other's eyes. They seemed poised and at home, though the whispers at all the other tables were about the Lewinsky charges. No pride? Or perhaps too much pride? But there in the shadow of Abraham Lincoln they carried on with dignity and good humor.

Despite all, they were a practiced couple on the presidential stage ... No pride? Or too much pride? They carried on with dignity and good humor

He had the good sense to retain Republican appointee Alan Greenspan as head of the Federal Reserve Board; his own Secretary of the Treasury, Robert Rubin, was a man of equal talent. Between this pair and Clinton's hands-off attitude, the U.S. economy soared to unimagined records for innovation and production of wealth. That seemingly illusive balanced federal budget actually became a fact under Clinton, and the nation could even scratch its head and ponder what to do with budget surpluses.

While Clinton's grasp of foreign policy at first seemed limited, he did make substantial progress for peace in the Middle East and in Northern Ireland. He took a lenient view of China as that country struggled to join the free market world. Later on, his anguished and unpopular decision to bomb in Kosovo brought at least a temporary end to the province's unspeakable and tragic "ethnic cleansing" and also silenced a chorus of prominent critics.

When Clinton won re-election in 1996, he seemed to be moving out of the dark shadows of his first term. Then he was struck by the sexual scandal involving a 21-year-old White

About the time that most of us thought we had run through all the possible surprises the Clinton Administration could offer, Hillary decided to run for the U.S. Senate representing New York State and shortly went house hunting in Chappaqua, vowing to split her time between the White House and the new suburban residence.

In his last months in office, Clinton acknowledged he was in a melancholy state of mind. "I'm going to miss this house," he said many times about the executive mansion. He talked of his new appreciation for the men whose pictures hung on the walls, of a sharpened sense of history, which he loved so much. But most of the time Bill Clinton was a nomad, drifting around the world and his country in Air Force One, attending summit meetings and fund raisers for the Democratic Party and its presumed presidential candidate in 2000, Vice President Al Gore. Clinton as often as not was off the front pages as the nation focused on a new election, a new President and a new century. It was a twilight time, but that is the way Thomas Jefferson and all those other "friends of Bill" meant it to be. ∎

1960

1963

1964

1975

1978

ARKANSAS BOY Bill Clinton was born William Jefferson Blythe 4th on August 19, 1946, in Hope, Arkansas. His father, W.J. Blythe 3rd, an auto-parts salesman, was killed in a car wreck before Bill was born. His mother Virginia, a nurse, married Roger Clinton in 1950 and moved to Hot Springs. Bill took his stepfather's name; halfbrother Roger was born in 1956. At age 14, Bill confronted his stepfather, a problem drinker, helping end abuse of his mother.

STANDOUT From grade school on, Clinton was a star student; by high school he was a frequent speaker to local community groups. In July 1963, he went to Washington as an Arkansas representative to Boys Nation, where he met his hero, John Kennedy, in the White House Rose Garden.

The Comeback Kid

WASHINGTON Clinton played sax in the high school band and was its manager. Aiming for a career in government, he attended Georgetown University in Washington, worked in the office of Arkansas Senator William Fulbright and campaigned for Democrats in Arkansas.

MARRIAGE A top student and campus leader in college, Clinton was named a Rhodes scholar and began studies at Oxford University in 1968. Avoiding the draft during the Vietnam War, he created a problem for his political future. After Oxford, he attended the Law School at Yale University, where he met Hillary Rodham; they wed in 1975.

POLITICS Back in Arkansas, Clinton taught law, lost a run for Congress in 1974, became attorney general in 1976 and was elected Governor in 1978, at only 32, left. Turned out by voters in 1980, he won the first of three more gubernatorial races in 1982.

1995

Triumph and Terrorism

Bill Clinton's America boomed with new technology but was torn by violence

1999

1998

1995

LOOKING INWARD: With the cold war over at last, Americans under Bill Clinton became preoccupied with domestic concerns (including those of the President, caught in a White House sex scandal in his second term). The ongoing technological revolution embodied by the Internet drove an economic surge that saw the creation of vast new wealth and many new jobs but culminated in the government's 1998 antitrust suit against Microsoft, headed by billionaire Bill Gates (left).

The good news about the economy was offset by a wave of domestic terrorism. Antigovernment bombers killed 168 innocent people at a federal office building in Oklahoma City in 1995, and a rash of school shootings peaked in Littleton, Colorado, in 1999, when two students killed 13 people (below). The much-watched 1995 trial of former football hero O.J. Simpson for the murder of his wife became a circus that fueled racial tensions and eroded respect for the law.

Abroad, the republics of the former Yugoslavia flared with ethnic violence through the '90s. When Serb strongman Slobodan Milosevic forced ethnic Albanians from Kosovo in 1999 (far left), Clinton helped lead NATO allies in an air war that restored them to their homeland.

1996

1999

Home Sweet White House

I have always taken a close look at the White House rooms when a new President arrives. Little things flesh out the story of a man and his family and his meaning. The past speaks to every President. There may not be a true Lincoln ghost that walks the corridors at night. But there is a true feeling of Lincoln's presence, from paintings and busts and books, that never leaves the White House.

HOUSE NOTES: LOOKING UP AT BILL AND HILLARY Clinton in the soft glow of the State Dining Room, Abraham Lincoln watching in oil. Clintons both beam, seem to want to keep the lease, giving contributors and helpers in the latest White House refurbishing a tour of the place and telling them of their joy at living there. It is leavening and deepening to be with memories of the greats, says Bill. Hillary has read bios on all the former First Ladies, keeps William Seale's *The President's House*—two volumes of rich history—handy and well thumbed. Bill can even recite some of the house's stories as well as the guides. "There isn't much job security in my line of work," he deadpans. "I may need the skill."

Guests go in clusters from Oval Office to Bill's private study. New paint, new carpets, new picture hangings everywhere as Little Rock decorator Kaki Hockersmith's means of making the house a Clinton home. Lincoln bust looks over Bill's desk in the Oval Office. Another Lincoln bust guards the office door. Lincoln's speeches lie between covers. Lincoln's a Republican; what is this? Nothing new. As noted by Harvard's David Donald, "Getting right with Lincoln" is standard for Presidents. Anyway, balance is restored over on the grand staircase in the mansion. Tucked nearly out of view is this Republican quartet— Harding, Hoover, Nixon and Reagan.

The new Oval Office blue carpet is deep, dramatic. "It's so masculine," said Chelsea when she first saw it. Clinton's favorite painting, Childe Hassam's *Avenue in the Rain,* a scene of misty flags, is a softer image that hangs on the curved wall. Most dramatic change: Treaty Room turned into deep red and burgundy study for Bill. Heavy thinking here. Nine books piled on the work area. Unlit cigar waiting for a flameless draw. Surely he lights up secretly in a chamber that once was continually beclouded by Ulysses Grant? Nope. Bill is famously allergic to smoke. New checkers and backgammon game tables suggest his indulgences. Heavy, historic desk was moved to the lawn for recent P.L.O.-Israel peace signing. President's personal possessions emptied from drawers. Now he can't find them all. *Hill-l-ar-r-ry!* On the wall is the famous photo by George Tames, New York *Times* photographer: Kennedy's back silhouetted as he leans to read newspapers in the Oval Office.

Heartbeat of the White House may come from the tiny private kitchen. Three Clintons can just fit. Hillary says they go there to dodge the din, sip, nibble, talk, hug. Hillary too busy for much home cooking. Bill can use the microwave; call Domino's.

New people, new decorations, new rituals. Still, a mallard came back again this year as a yard guest, built a nest in a 160-year-old elm tree down near the tennis court, hatched 11 ducklings. Just flew south for the winter season untroubled by trade, taxes or health care. ∎

COMPARE AND CONTRAST George Bush's Oval Office is at left; Bill Clinton's redecorated version of the room is on the right

The Curse of Good Times

In one of those curious events in my life of writing about Presidents, Bill Clinton told me he had taken a new interest in the presidency of Rutherford B. Hayes—two years after this column appeared. Was he a secret reader, or had the lack of opportunity for heroics in his term simply led him to find a kindred spirit in the history books? Someday I'll ask him.

IVY LEAGUE LAWYER IN THE OVAL OFFICE, BRILLIANT political practitioner, champion of better education for poor black children, husband of a woman who broke precedent and bravely crusaded nationally on one of the great social issues of the day, voracious book reader, shrewd observer who identified a massive shift in the U.S. economy and the job skills required to meet it, partisan of women's rights, winner of a knock-down, drag-out battle with a Congress that attempted to shut down the government and humiliate the President.

Bill Clinton? Not on your life. I'm talking about Rutherford B. Hayes, a President brushed aside by history and used as the prop of a thousand Washington toastmasters searching for a cheap laugh over the past 120 years. Humorist Bob Orben says the name is melodic ("Chester Arthur doesn't make it"), and Hayes' dim place in the national chronicle makes him fodder for jokes.

Clinton should take a lesson from Hayes if he wants to avoid being trapped by history into a forgettable presidency. His 19th century predecessor has been given a raw reading by historians who are just as enamored of wars and depressions and human calamity as Hollywood. They have tended to write bad scripts, at least at first, for those Presidents who presided in moments of prosperity and tranquillity and kept them that way. Cases in point: George Bush, Jimmy Carter, Dwight Eisenhower, William Howard Taft and Martin Van Buren.

High political priest of all historians Arthur Schlesinger Jr. assembled a jury a while back to judge presidential greatness. This flocking of fellow liberals naturally elevated John Kennedy and Lyndon Johnson and diminished Jerry Ford and Ronald Reagan. But the shocker was that Bill Clinton was also put down there with Hayes, Arthur and Benjamin Harrison and devastatingly close to Calvin Coolidge. The White House has not stopped quivering in indignation. Clinton's greatest second-term battle may be against historical irrelevance: there is ample evidence that he understands the difficulty of being a heroic leader in a democracy in a period of well-being and peace. No civil war, no winning of the West, no world wars (hot or cold), no depression, no Dust Bowl. Even Schlesinger admits democracies often are at their worst in good times.

Clinton will attempt to take the crisis in America's personal and cultural values, along with the great economic changes caused by an industrial society giving way to the information age, and weave everything into a coherent national challenge with the language of hope and inspiration. Only one President so far has managed to do that. He was the muscular Theodore Roosevelt—rancher, explorer, author,

HAYES Like Clinton, he lacked a major crisis to test his mettle

hunter, warrior—who defined by his intelligence and personal exuberance America's arrival as the world's greatest mover and shaker. But even T.R. confessed that his success was based on the fact that the U.S. was in a "heroic mood." Is the nation now closer to Hayes or Roosevelt? And can it be nudged ahead?

"Modern historians like crisis management, crisis response and presidential swashbuckling," says Richard Norton Smith, a biographer of George Washington's. "My reading of Rutherford B. Hayes is that he was a great man who was President at a time when greatness lay beyond the presidency—in Congress and in the private sector." That situation exists in this nation today.

Other historical similarities between the Hayes and Clinton eras are startling. A Europe beginning a 40-year interlude of peace (for Clinton, read as the end of the cold war). A nation changing from an agricultural economy to an industrial base (now, industry to information). A First Lady, "Lemonade Lucy," devoted to attacking the great social and family scourge of alcohol (not far removed from Hillary's health-care and children's crusades).

If Clinton can deliver on the prosaic aspects of government (Social Security, a balanced budget, education), he may climb up beside Roosevelt. "Clinton," says historian Smith, "needs to decide what needs to be done in this country, and he needs to just do it. If he starts to poll historians about what to do, he probably will never make it." ■

Picture Credits

Credits read clockwise from top left.

Cover Michael Evans-Sygma, AP/Wide World, Cecil Stoughton-John F. Kennedy Library, Don Carl Steffan-TIME Magazine, Owen Franken-Corbis Sygma, Robert Knudson-The White House, Carl Iwasaki-Life, AP/Wide World, Cynthia Johnson, P.F. Bentley

Back Cover/Title Page Cynthia Johnson

Table of Contents iii Courtesy Hugh Sidey

Introduction vi-vii Courtesy Hugh Sidey (8)

Roosevelt 2 Franklin D. Roosevelt Library **4** Marie Hansen-LIFE **5** no credit, Franklin D. Roosevelt Library, UPI/Corbis Bettmann, AP/Wide World (2) **6-7** News Photo, U.S. Navy, no credit, Dorothea Lange-National Archives, Keystone **8** Paul Dorsey-Pix Inc./Time Inc., Roddy E. Mims-Time Inc. **9** R. Ellis-Corbis Sygma

The People's Choice 10-11 Raymond Depardon-Magnum **12** David Hume Kennerly-The White House **13** Cynthia Johnson **14** UPI/Corbis Bettmann **15** Peter Stackpole-LIFE **16** Bill Beebe-Los Angeles *Times* **17** David Tulis-Atlanta *Journal Constitution* **18-19** Bill Pierce **20** Arthur Grace-Corbis Sygma, AP/Wide World **21** UPI/Corbis Bettmann

Truman 22 AP/Wide World **24** UPI/Corbis Bettmann **25** Harry S. Truman Library (4), W. Eugene Smith-LIFE **26** Triangle Photos, Y. Matsushige, U.S. Army **27** Army-Navy Task Force, Walter Sanders-LIFE, Major R.V. Spencer-USAF/National Archives, Robert Clover-AP/Wide World, **28** UPI/Corbis Bettmann **29** George Skadding-LIFE

Backstage Pass 30-31 Dennis Brack-Black Star **32** Ed Clark-LIFE **33** Ed Clark-LIFE **34** Yoichi Okamoto-Lyndon B. Johnson Library **35** Yoichi Okamoto-Lyndon B. Johnson Library **36** David Valdez-George Bush Presidential Library **37** David Burnett-Contact **38** no credit **39** Pete Souza-The Ronald Reagan Library

Eisenhower 40 Michael Rougier-LIFE **42** Ed Clark-LIFE **43** no credit (2), INP/Corbis Bettmann, Lt. Moore-U.S. Army/National Archives, Carl Iwasaki-LIFE **44** Andrew St. George, Michael Rougier-LIFE, Hank Walker-LIFE, TASS/Sovfoto **45** John Bryson-Time Inc., Francis Miller-LIFE **46** AP/Wide World **47** UPI/Corbis Bettmann

Inner Circle 48-49 UPI/Corbis Bettmann **50** Robert Burgess **51** UPI/Corbis Bettmann **52-53** David Valdez-George Bush Presidential Library **54** Diana Walker **55** Hank Walker-LIFE **56** Yoichi Okamoto-Lyndon B. Johnson Library, Rowland Scherman-Time Inc. **57** John Zimmerman-TIME Magazine **58** Acme **59** David Hume Kennerly-The White House

Kennedy 60 Cecil Stoughton-John F. Kennedy Library **62** Art Rickerby-LIFE **63** John F. Kennedy Library (2), Yale Joel-LIFE, John F. Kennedy Library (2) **64** Paul Schutzer-LIFE, Documentation Roger Pic **65** U.S. Defense Department, Walter Sanders-Black Star, John Dominis-LIFE, John F. Kennedy Library **66** Paul Schutzer-LIFE **67** Fred H. Brandy

At Ease 68-69 Yoichi Okamoto-Lyndon B. Johnson Library **70** Carl Iwasaki-Time Inc. **71** AP/Wide World **72** AP/Wide World, Robert L. Knudson-John F. Kennedy Library **73** P.F. Bentley **74-75** Eddie Adams **76** Bill Hudson-AP/Wide World **77** Ed Clark-LIFE, Susan Biddle-Ronald Reagan Library **78** AP/Wide World **79** David Hume Kennerly-The White House

Johnson 80 Don Carl Steffen-TIME Magazine **82** George Silk-LIFE **83** Lyndon B. Johnson Library (3), AP/Wide World, Yoichi Okamoto-Lyndon B. Johnson Library **84** David Douglas Duncan, Co Rentmeester **85** Steve Shapiro, Josef Koudelka-Magnum, Cecil W. Stoughton-Lyndon B. Johnson Library, Bill Eppridge-LIFE **86** Stan Wyman-LIFE **87** AP/Wide World

Commander in Chief 88-89 Diana Walker **90** Jack Kightlinger-Lyndon B. Johnson Library **91** AP/Wide World, Francis J. Grandy-*Stars & Stripes* **92** INP/Corbis Bettmann **93** Sam Schulman-INP/Corbis Bettmann **94-95** Harry S. Truman Library, Pictorial Parade-Archive, Lt. Victor Jorgensen-U.S. Navy, Cummings-Prentiss Studio, no credit (2) **96** Arthur Schatz-LIFE **97** Dirck Halstead

Nixon 98 Robert Knudson-The White House, **100** John Dominis-LIFE **101** UPI/Corbis Bettmann, Whittier College, Harris & Ewing, INP/Corbis Bettmann, AP/Wide World **102** Kent State University, John Dominis-LIFE, Dirck Halstead **103** NASA, Larry Burrows-LIFE **104** The White House **105** David Hume Kennerly

Ford 106 Ricardo Thomas-The White House **108** Dirck Halstead **109** no credit (4), Ollie Atkins-The White House **110** Thai Khac Chuong-UPI/Corbis Bettmann, U.S. Navy, Ed Streeky-Time Inc. **111** Ortiz-Sander-Gailway Graphics, Boston *Globe*, NASA **112** AP/Wide World **113** Dirck Halstead

Puttin' on the Ritz 114-115 Paul Schutzer-LIFE **116** Hank Walker-LIFE **117** Franklin D. Roosevelt Library **118** Barbara Kinney-The White House **119** Michael Evans-The White House **120-121** AP/Wide World, The White House-AP/Wide World, Neshan Naltchayan-Reuters/Archive, Gerald R. Ford Library, George Bush Presidential Library **122** ©Mark Shaw-Photo Researchers **123** Hank Walker-LIFE **124** Paul Schutzer-LIFE **125** Diana Walker **126-127** Diana Walker

Carter 128 Jay Leviton-Atlanta **130** Kit Luce **131** AP/Wide World (2), no credit, Al Alexander-The Ledger-Enquirer Newspaper, George Tames-New York *Times* **132** Paola Ricci, Steve McCurry-Magnum **133** Robin Moyer-Liaison, Springmann-Black Star, Alain Mingam-Liaison, Mark Meyer **134** Frank Lerner-Metropolitan Museum of Art, AP/Wide World, Louis Fabian Bachrach **135** Karl Schumacher-The White House

This Old House 136-137 Ed & Mark Segal-Panoramic Images-Chicago **138** The Granger Collection, NY (2), ©Corbis, The Granger Collection, NY (2) **139** Harry S. Truman Library

Reagan 140 Michael Evans-Sygma **142** no credit **143** no credit (2), Photofest, Michael Evans-Liaison, Ron Edmonds-AP/Wide World **144** Dennis Brack-Black Star, James Nachtwey-Magnum, Susan Steinkamp-Saba **145** Peter Jordan, DeWildenberg-Liaison, Bruce Weaver-AP/Wide World, AP/Wide World **146** Paul Conrad-©1984 L.A. *Times* **147** Shalom Bar Tal-Yediot Achronot

On the Road 148-149 Ollie Atkins-The White House **150** Diana Walker **151** J. Scott Applewhite-AP/Wide World **152-153** David Hume Kennerly-The White House **154** David Hume Kennerly **155** Dennis Brack-Black Star **156** Peter Jordan **157** Aurore

Bush 158 Susan Biddle-George Bush Presidential Library **160** Diana Walker **161** no credit, George Bush Presidential Library, no credit (2), Cynthia Johnson **162** Charles Steiner-The Image Works, Kim Kulish-Los Angeles *Daily News*, Anthony Suau-Liaison **163** Stuart Franklin-Magnum, David Burnett-Contact, Alan Tannenbaum-Sygma, Ulli Michel-Reuters/Archive **164** Diana Walker **165** Doug Mills-AP/Wide World

Curtain Call 166-167 U.S. Parachuting Association **168** Francis Miller-LIFE **169** Steve McCurry-Magnum **170** George Tames-Time Inc. **171** Carl Mydans-LIFE **172-173** Michael Metcalf-Contact **174** Pete Souza-Ronald Reagan Library **175** Ed Clark-LIFE

Clinton 176 P.F. Bentley **178** Terry Ashe **179** no credit, Arnie Sachs-Corbis Sygma, no credit (2), Hank Wilson **180** Lisa Rudy Hoke-Black Star, Damir Sagolj-Reuters/Archive **181** AP/Wide World, Myung J. Chun-Pool, George Kochaniec-*Rocky Mountain News*, Dirck Halstead **182** Susan Biddle-The White House, Ping Amranand **183** Library of Congress